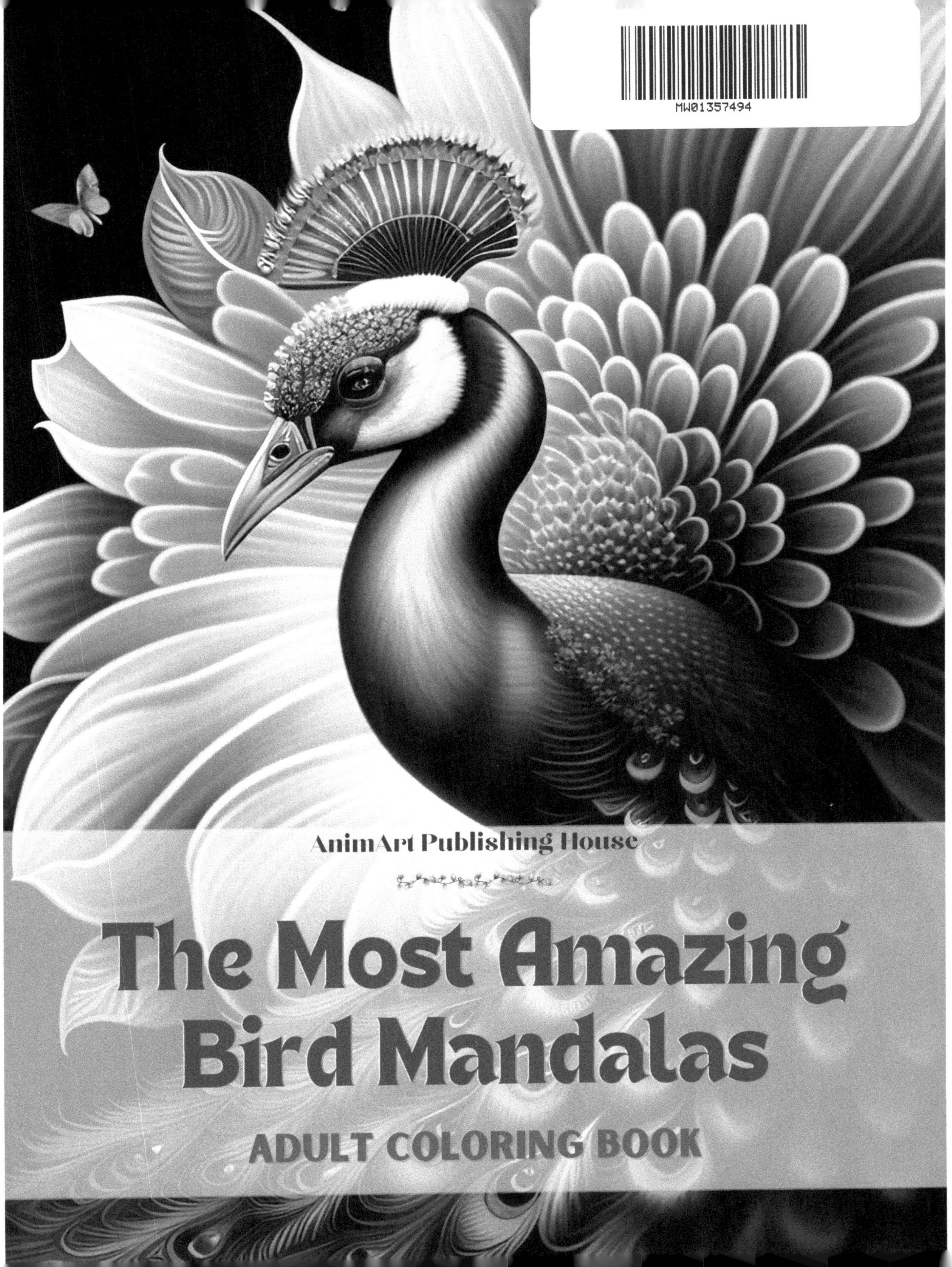

AnimArt Publishing House

The Most Amazing Bird Mandalas

ADULT COLORING BOOK

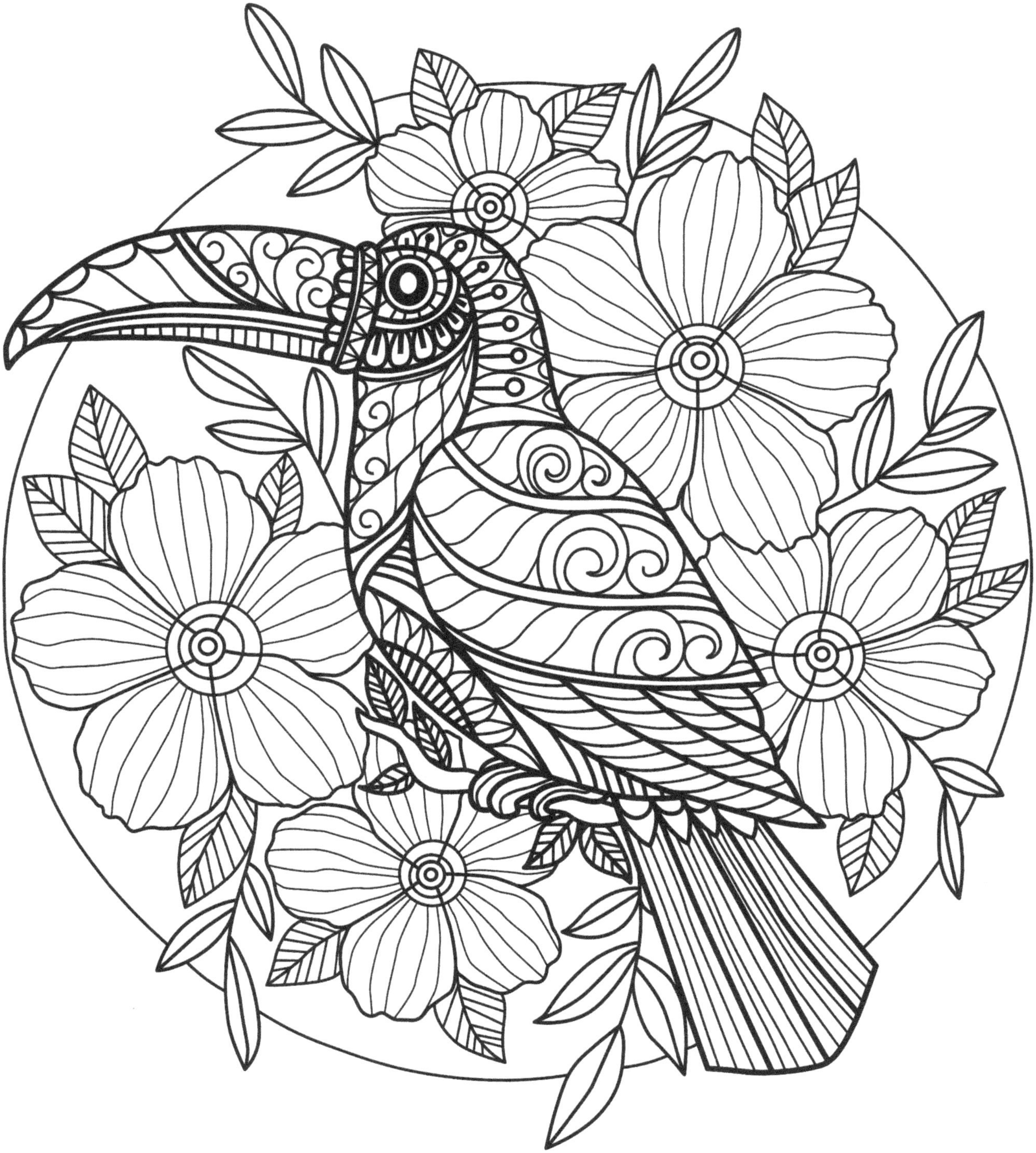

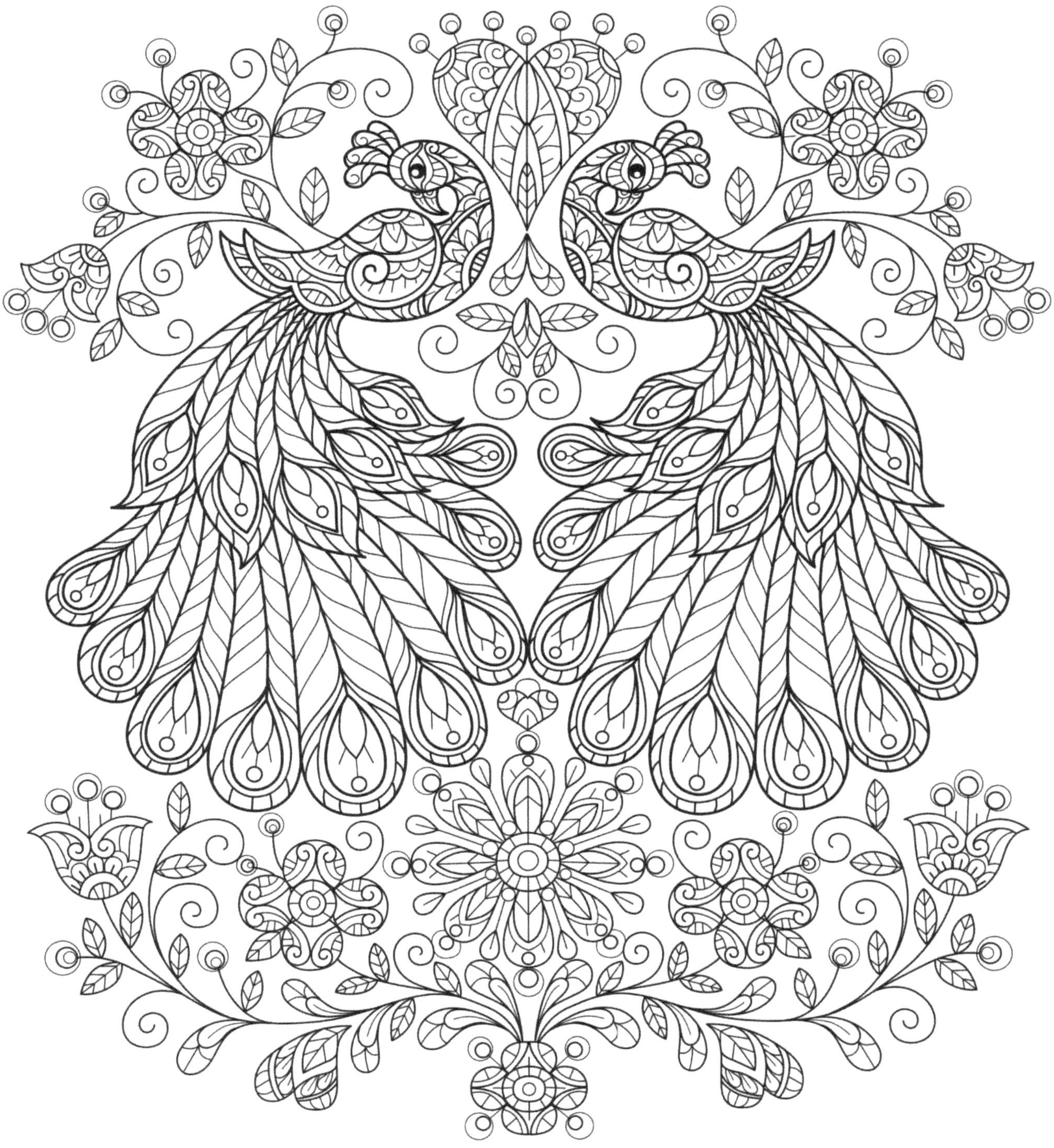

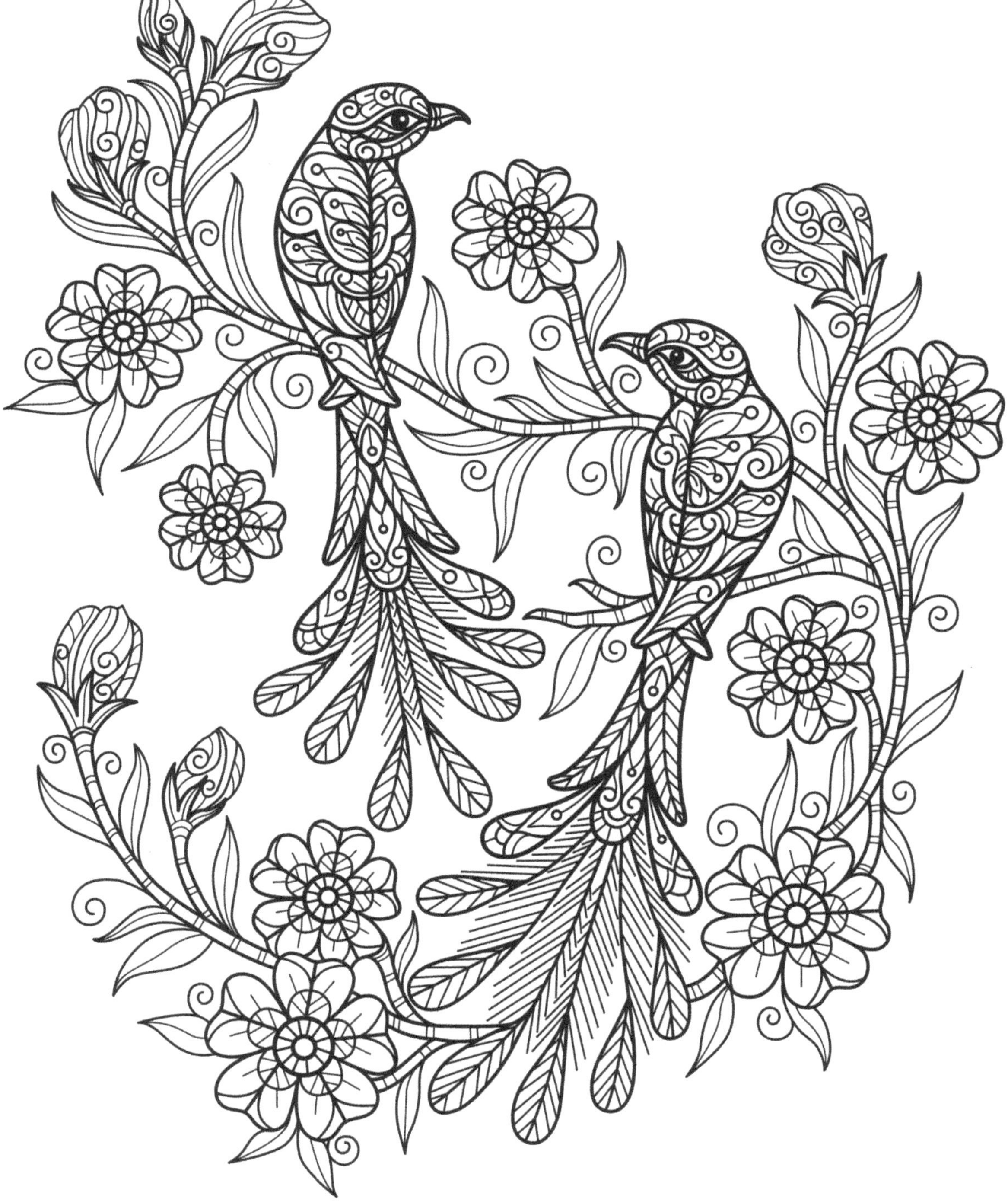

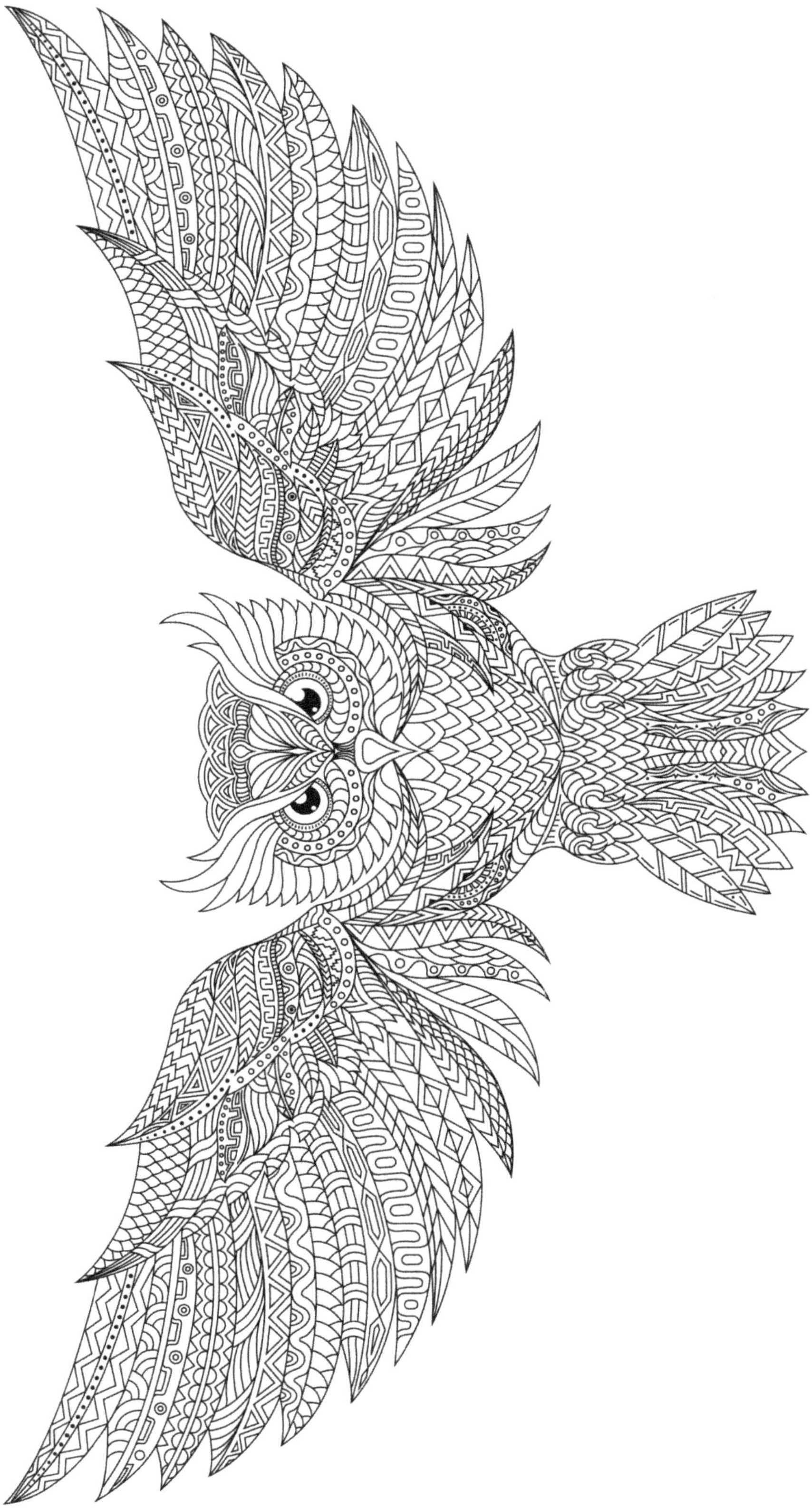

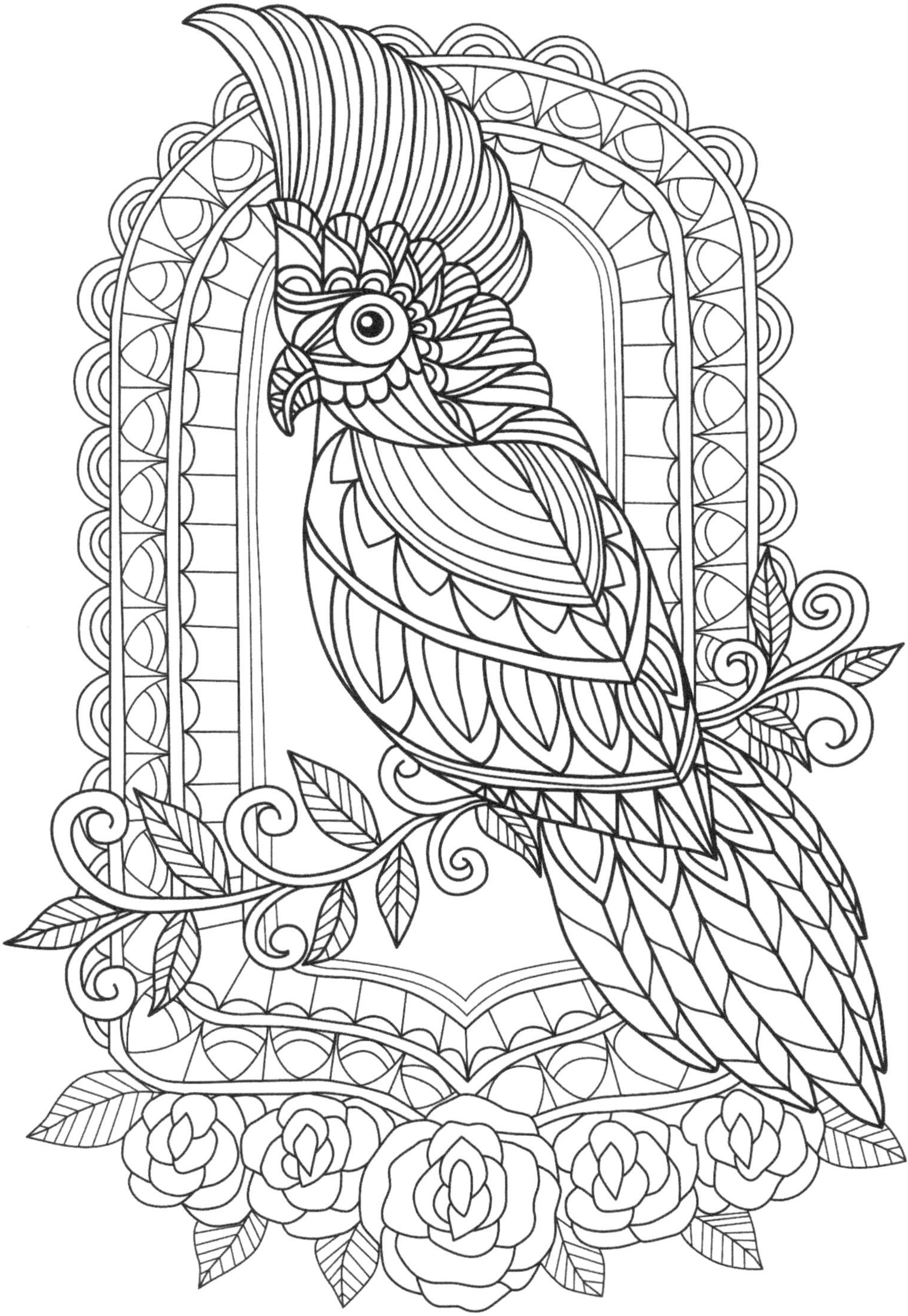

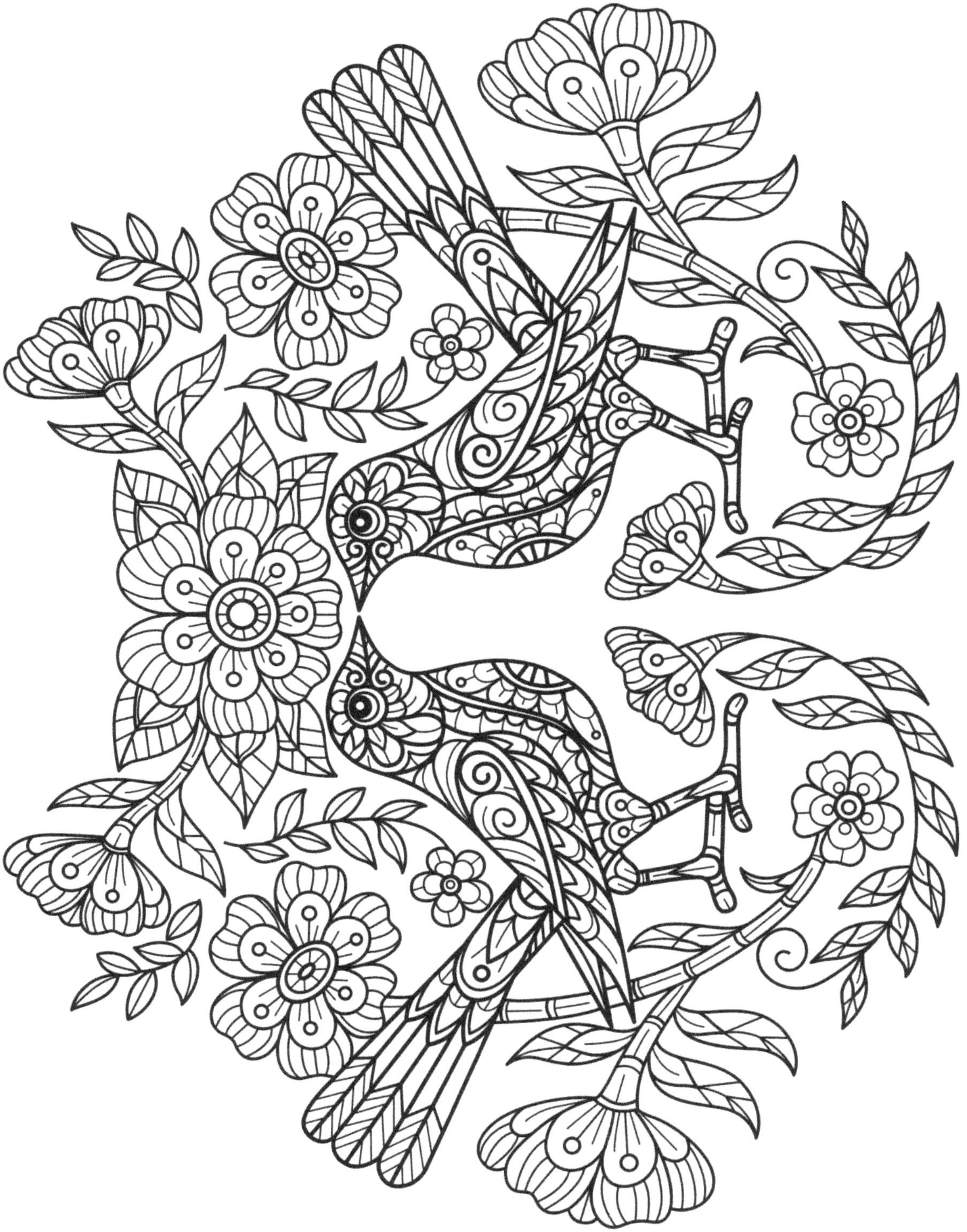

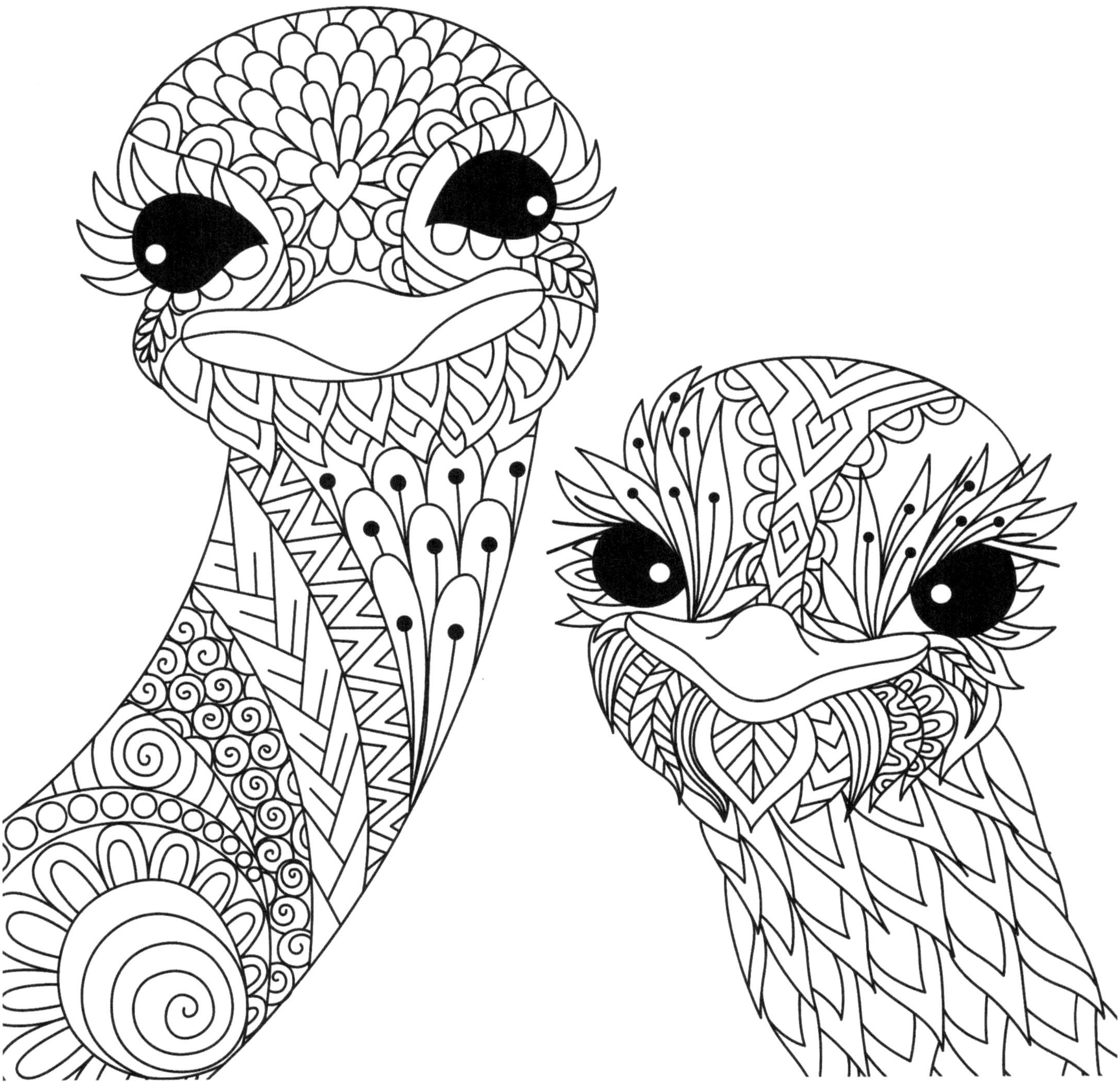

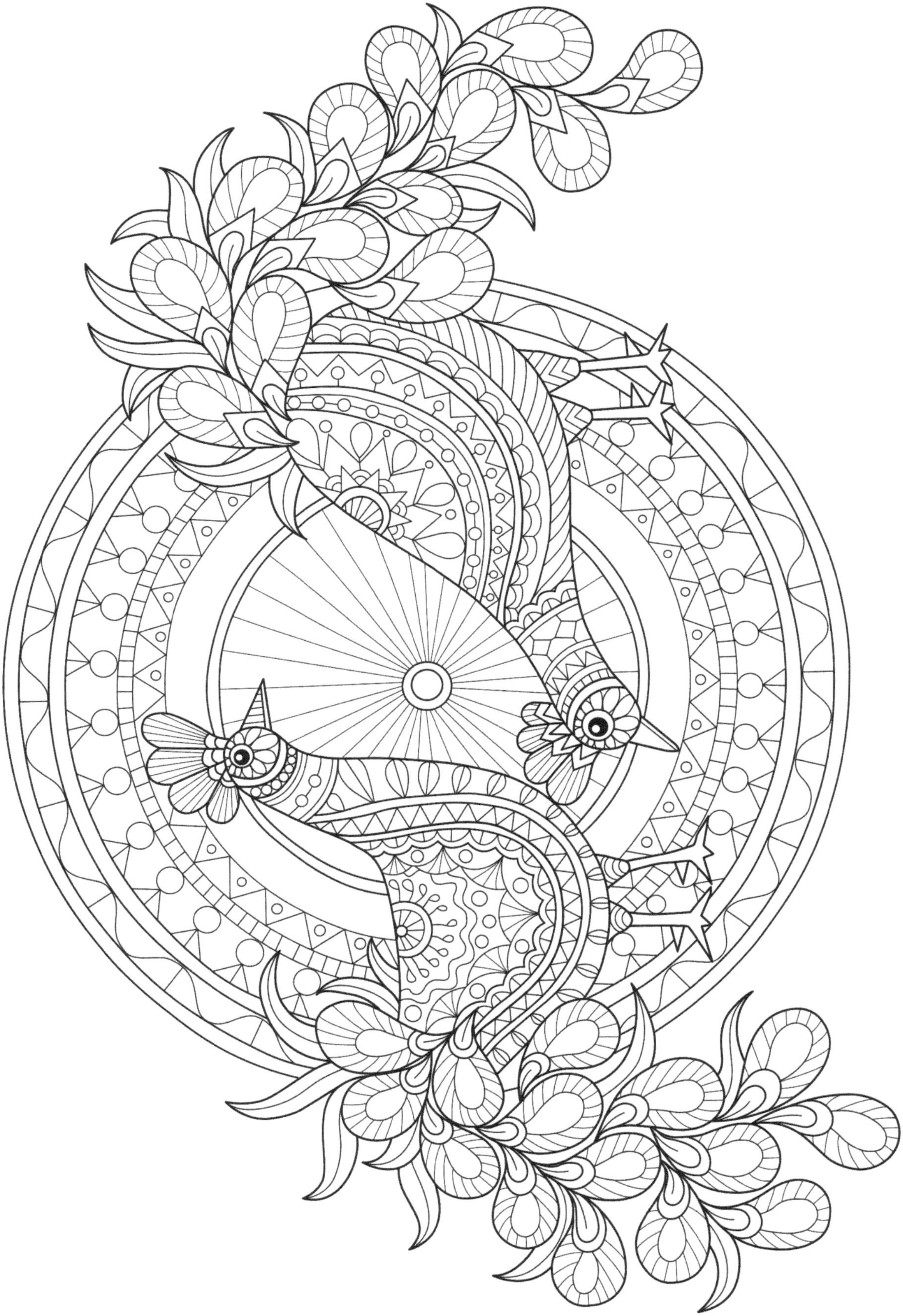

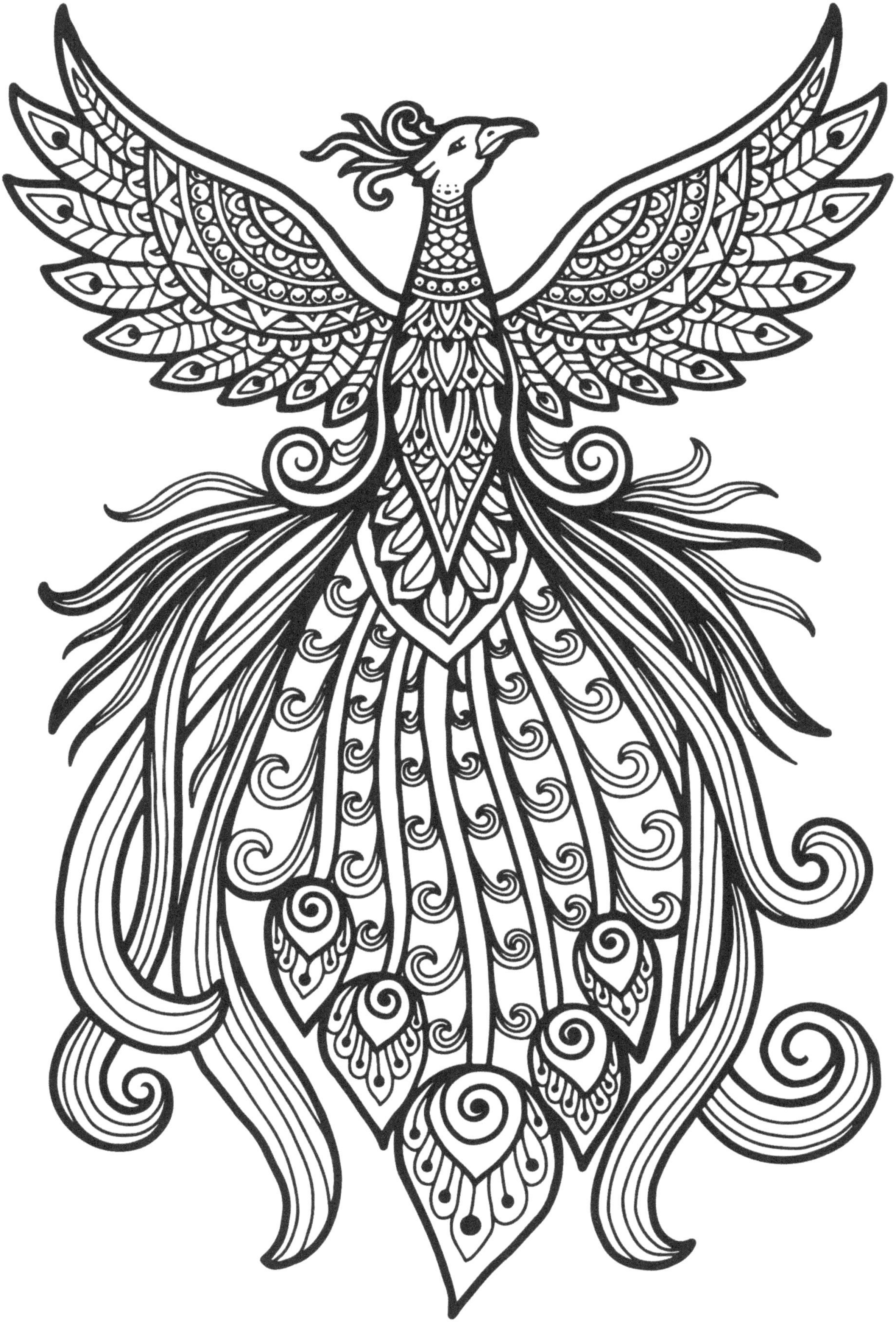

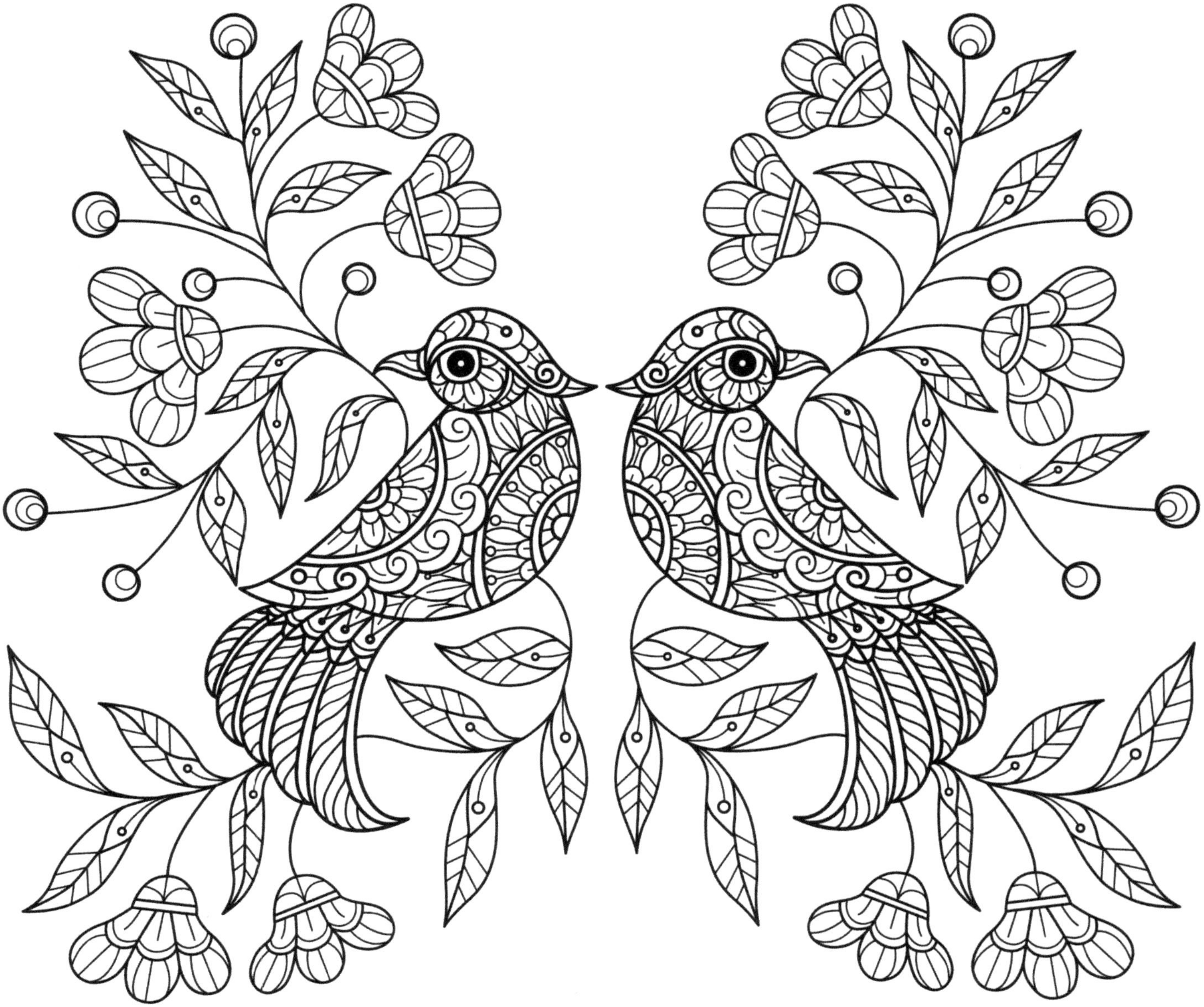

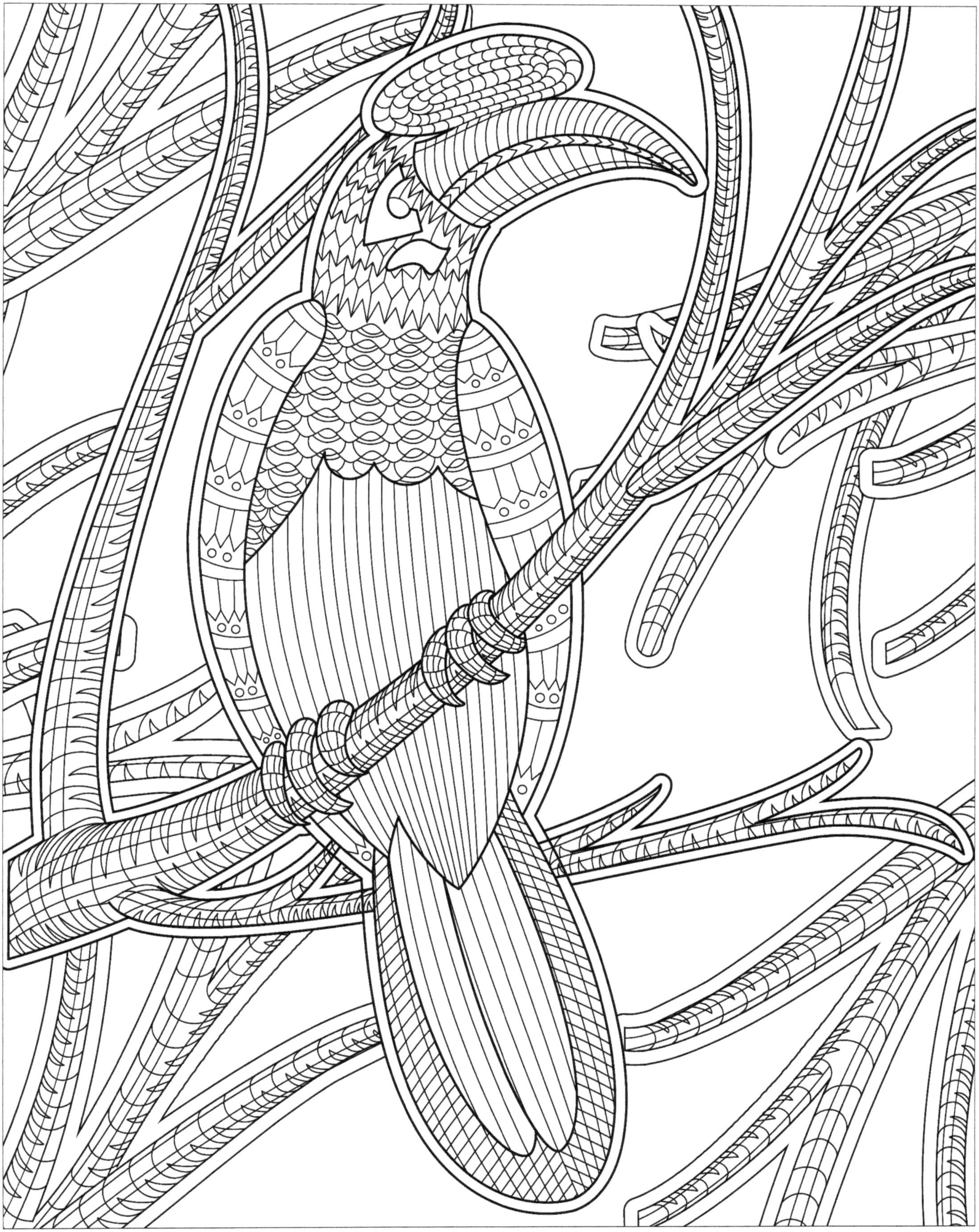

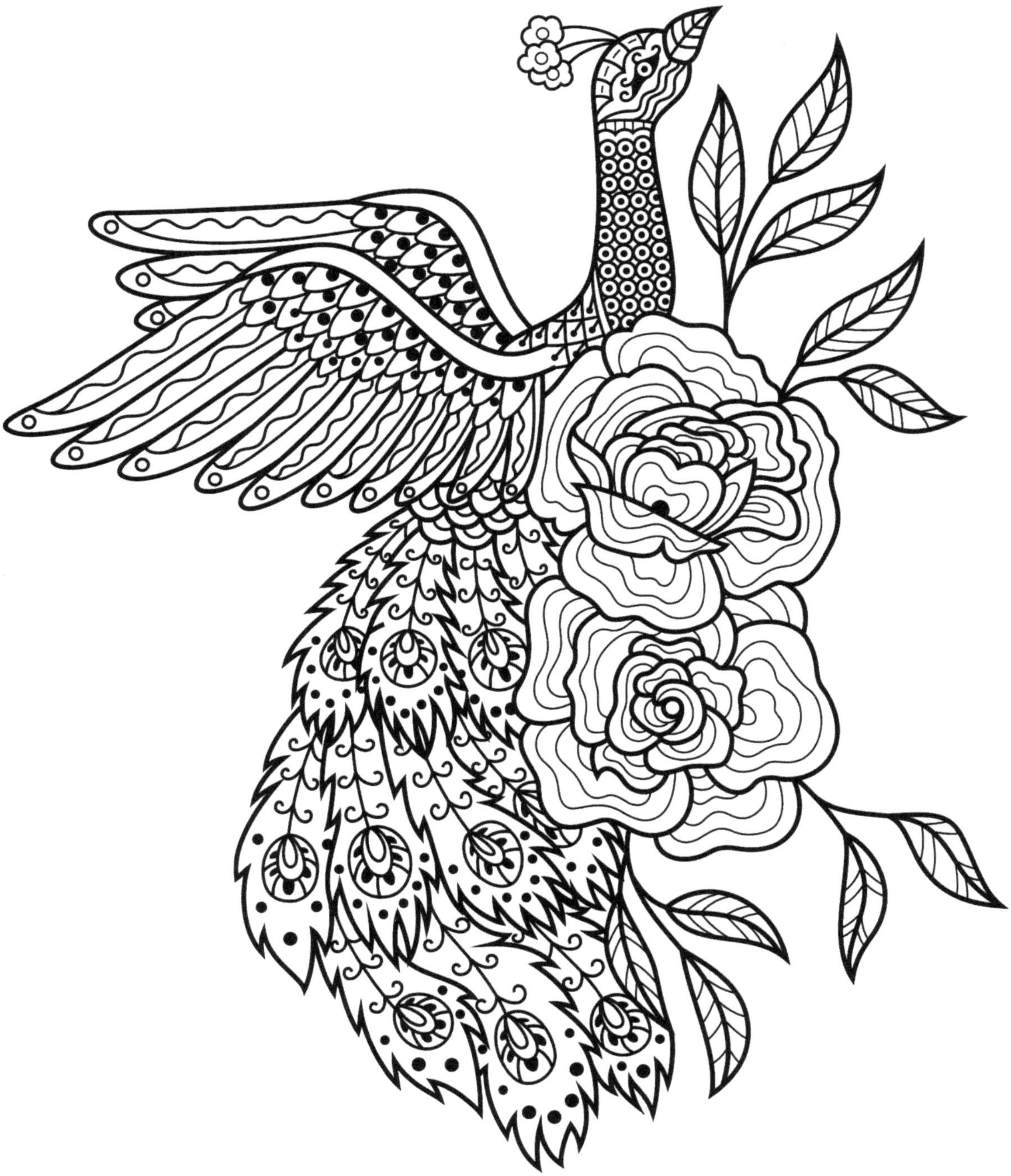

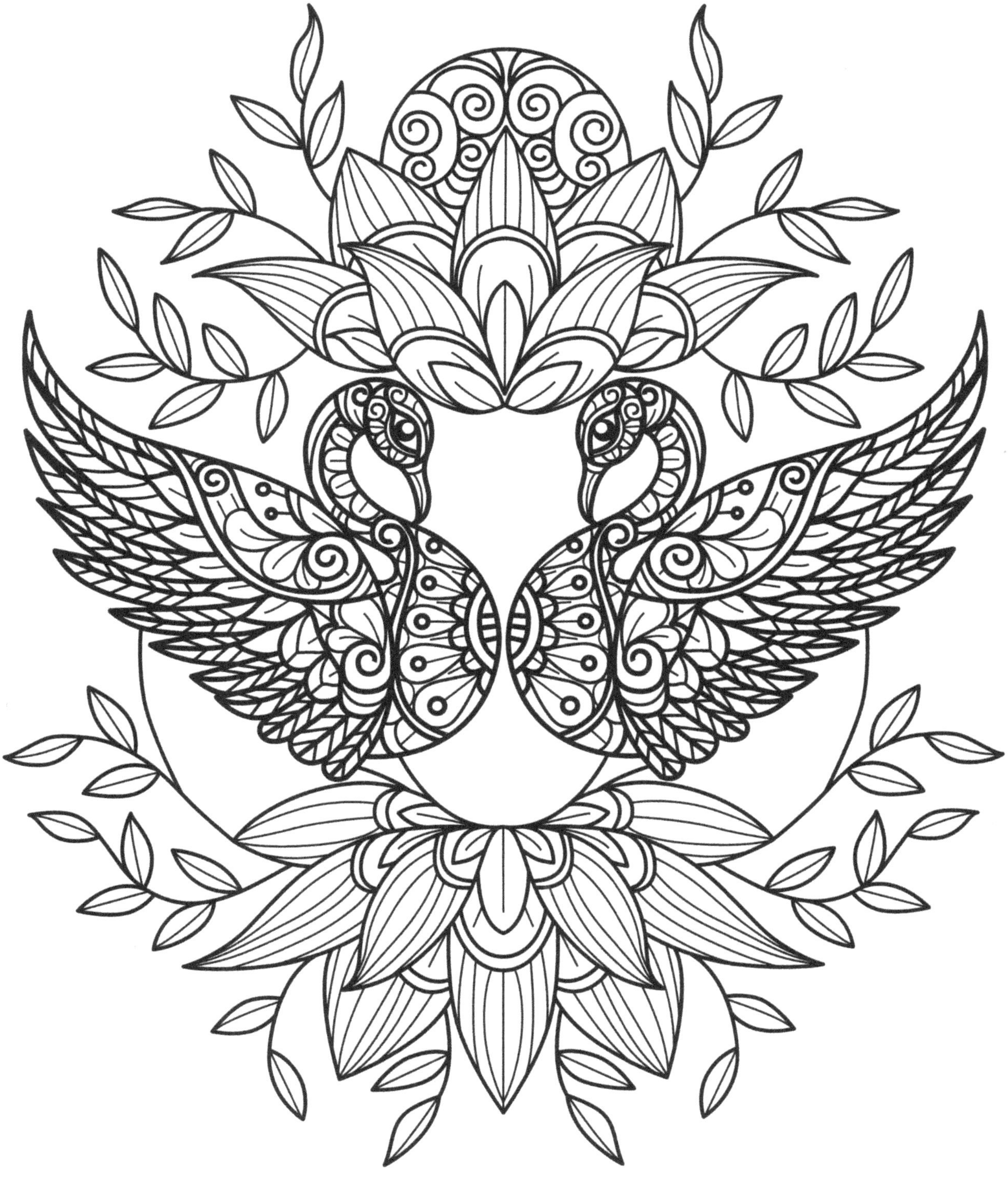

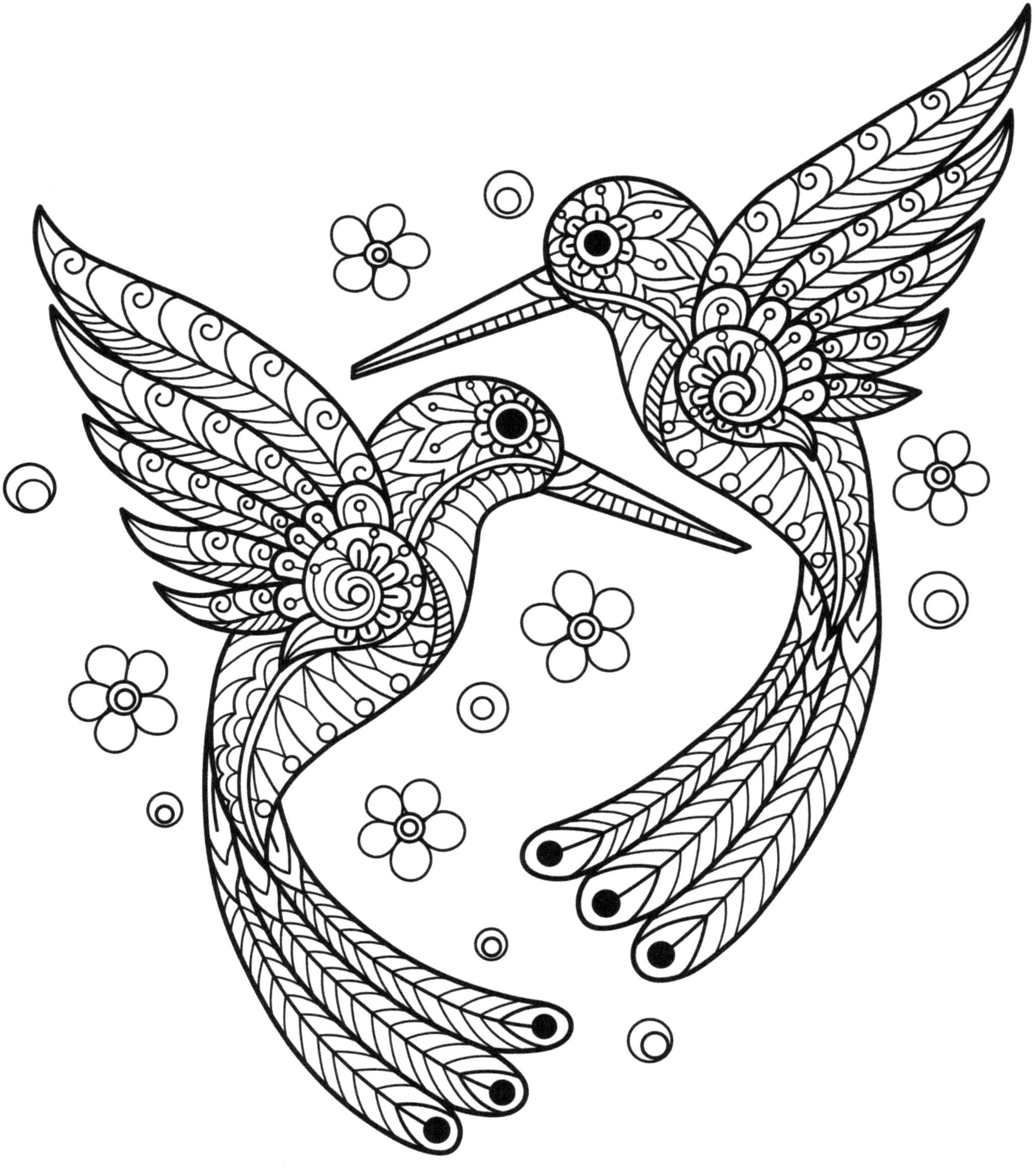

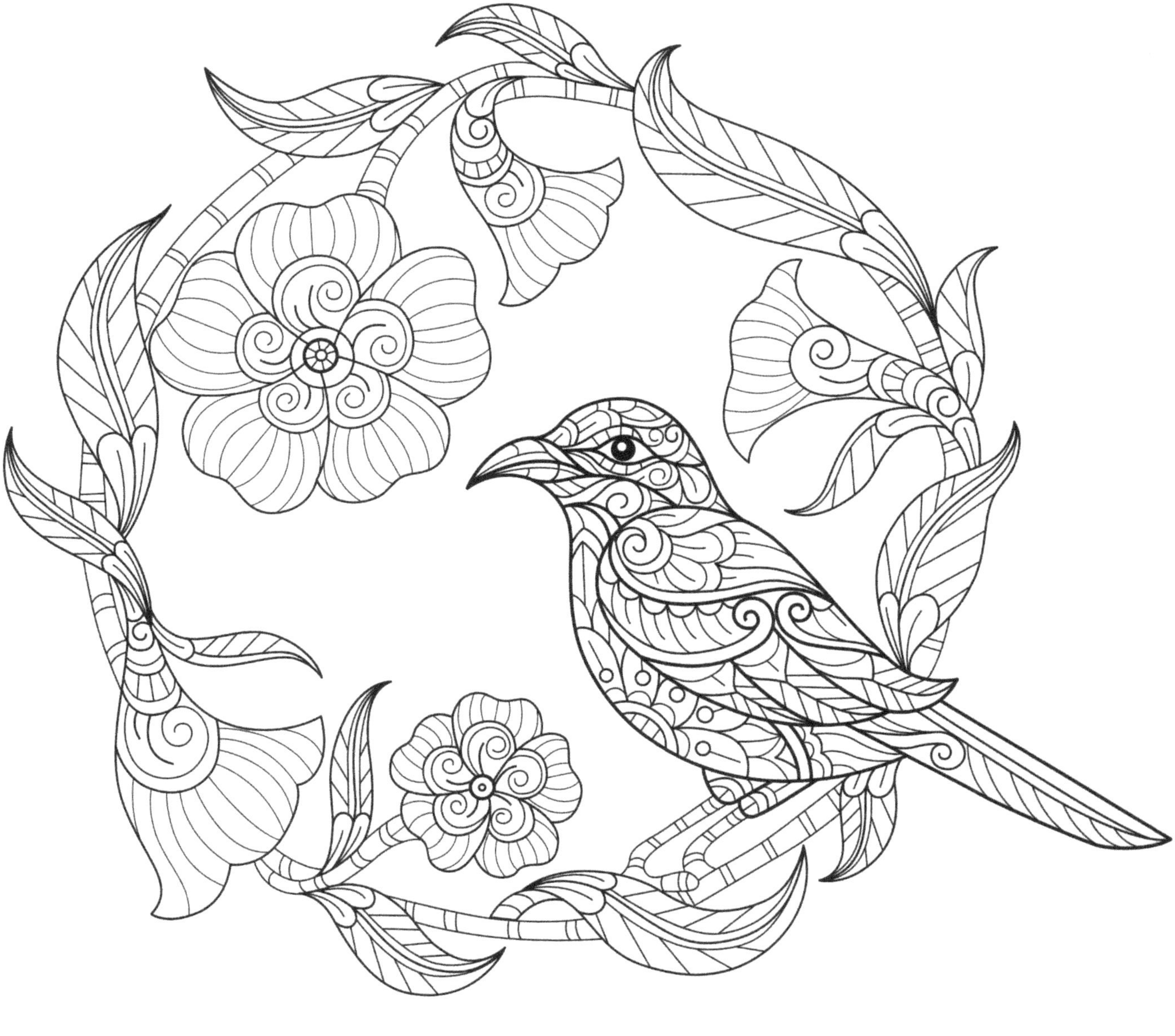

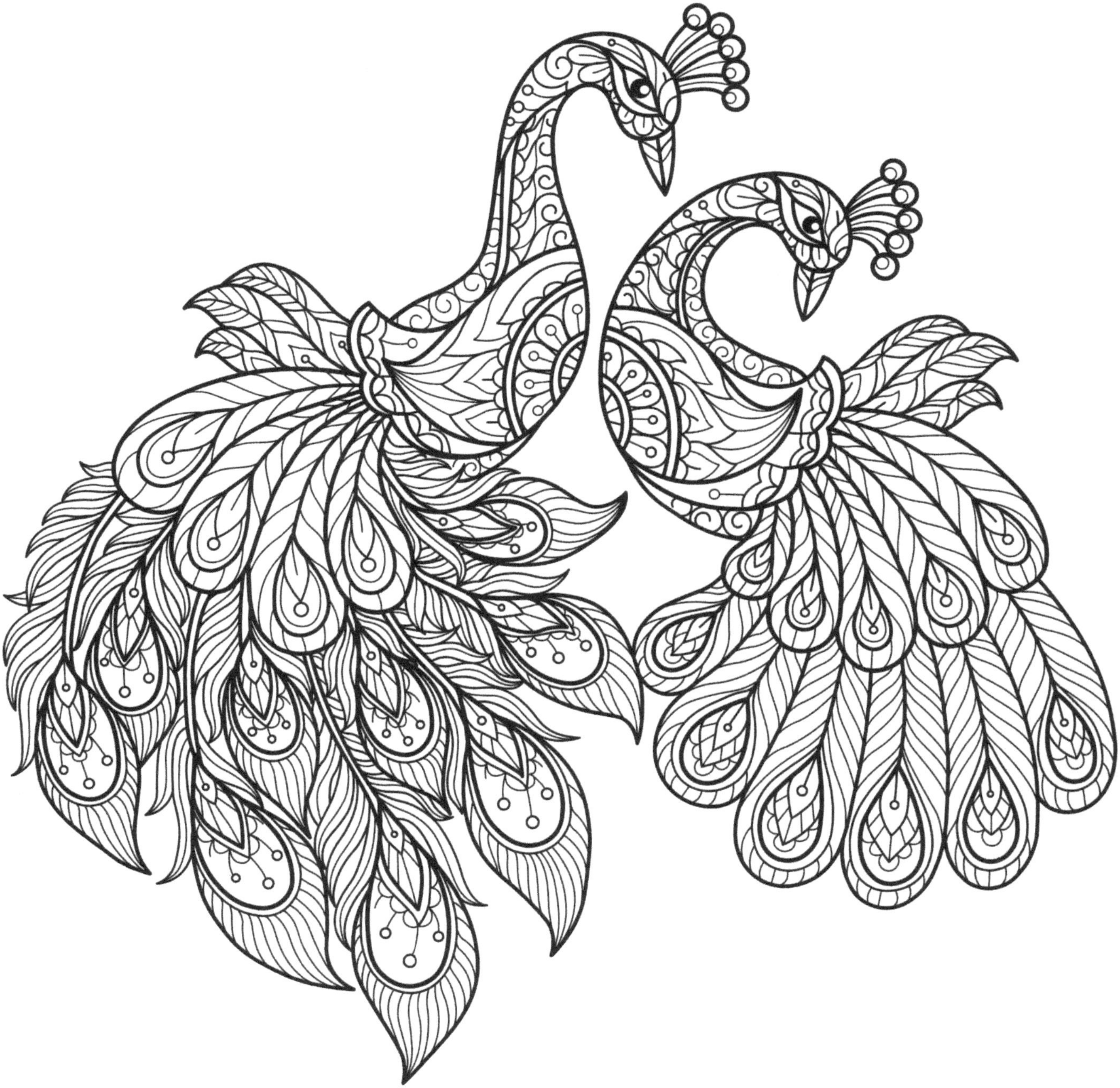

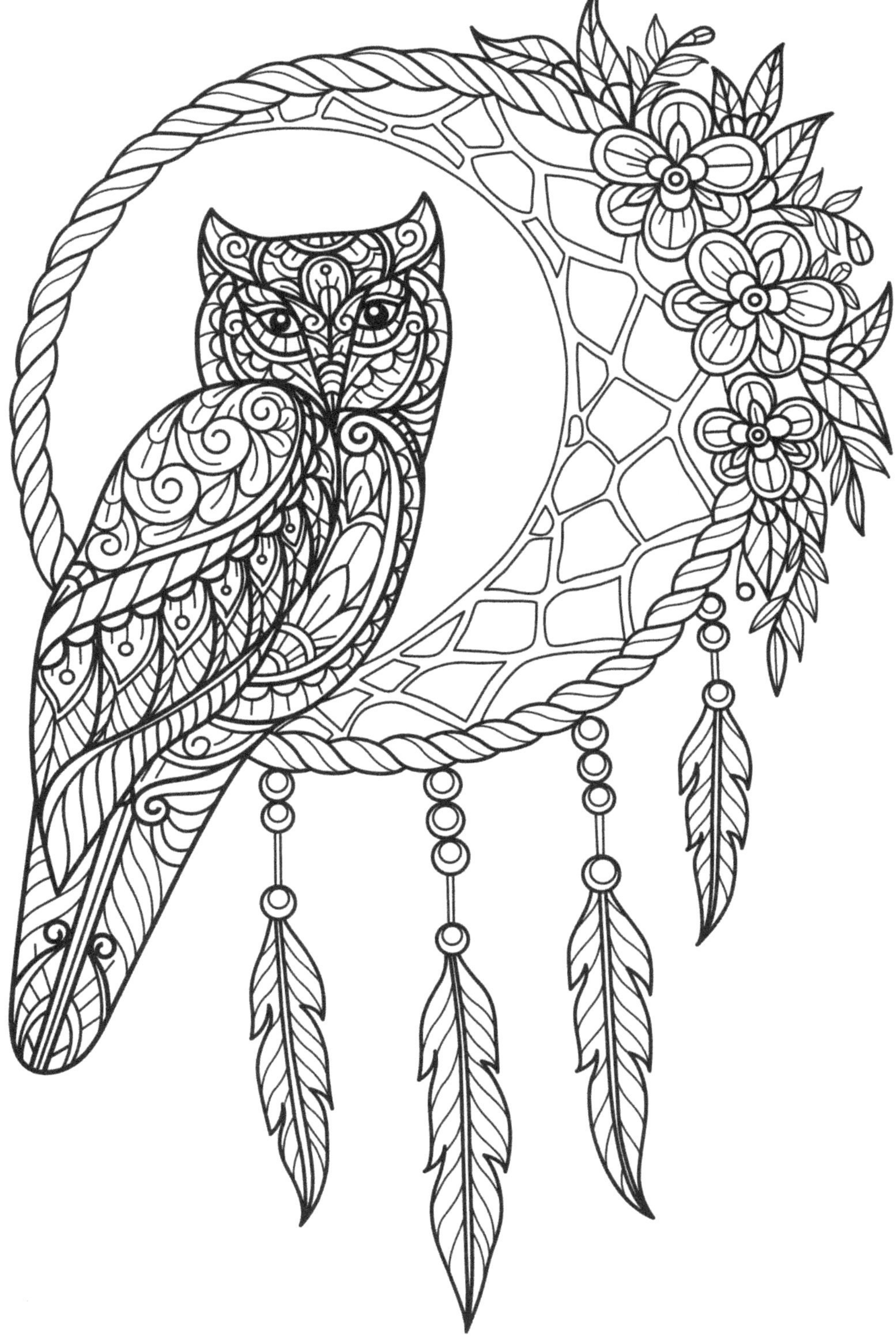

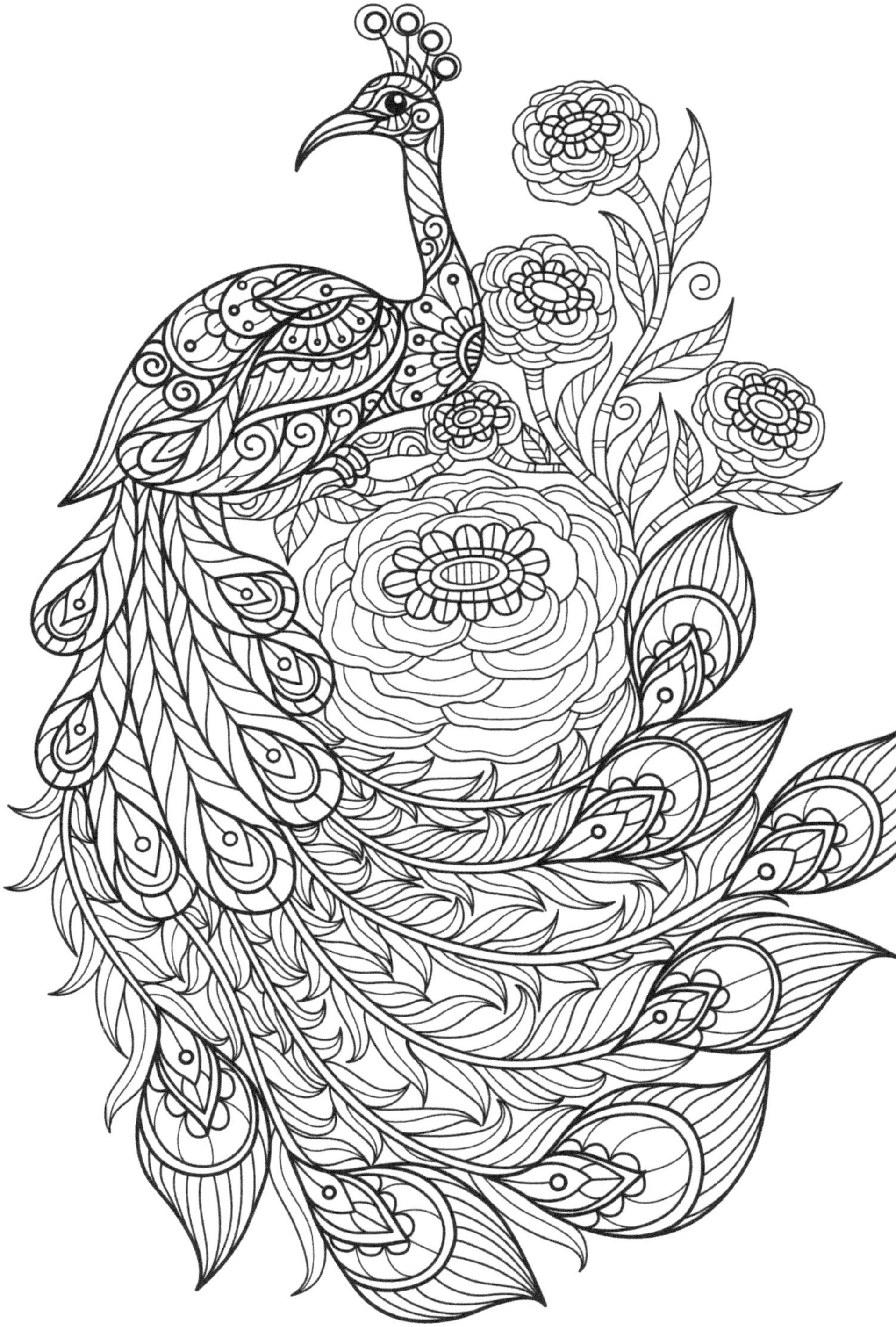

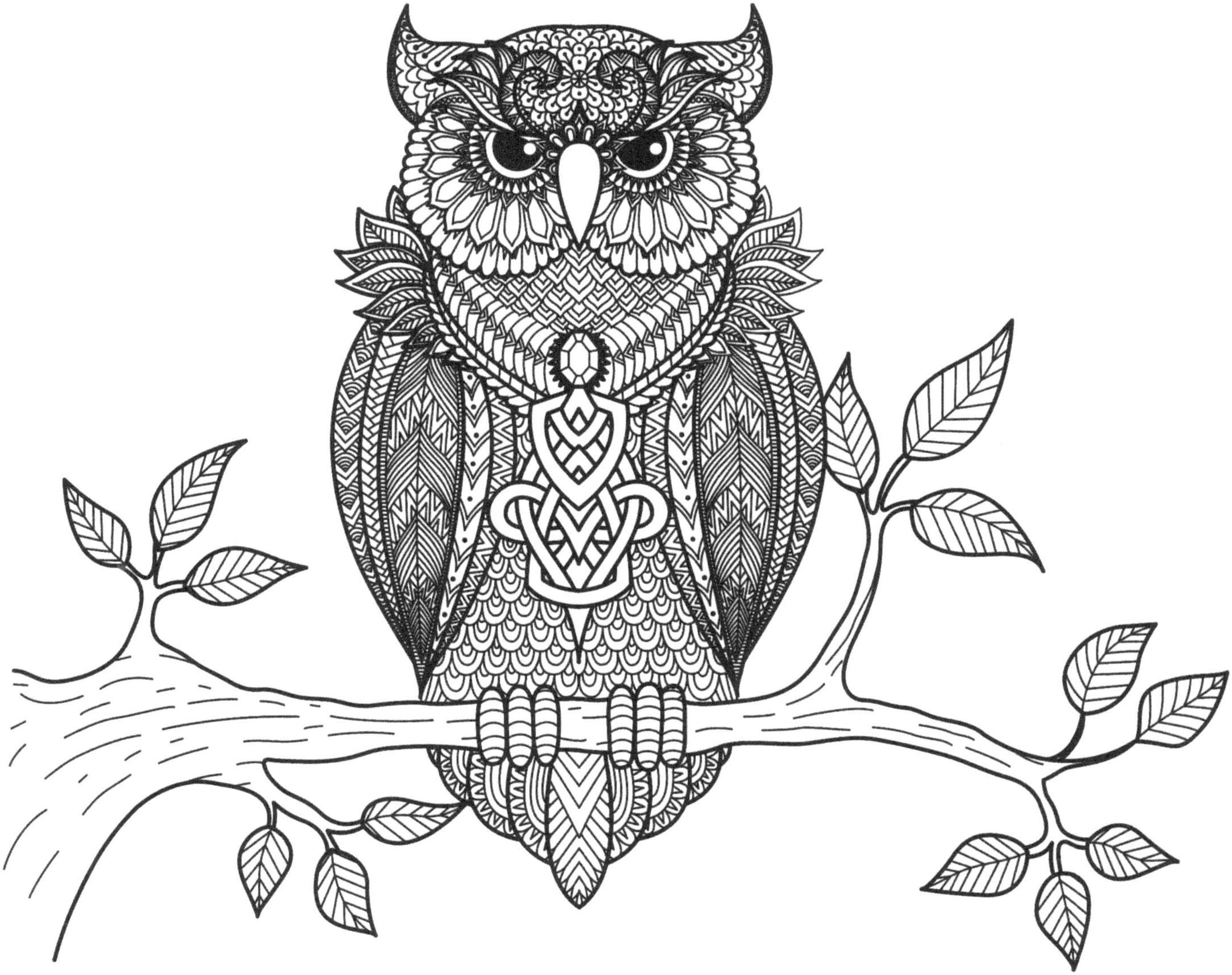

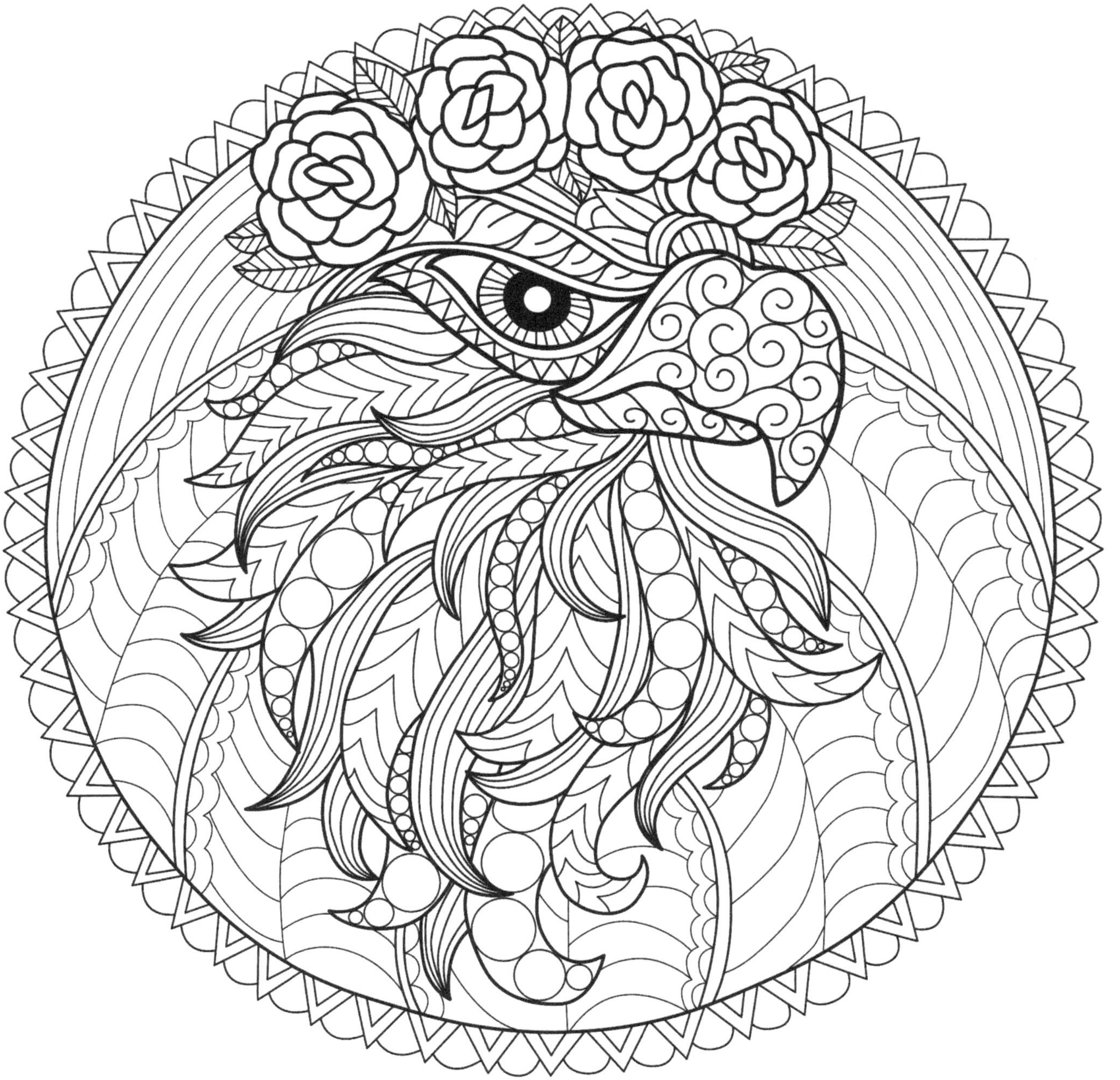

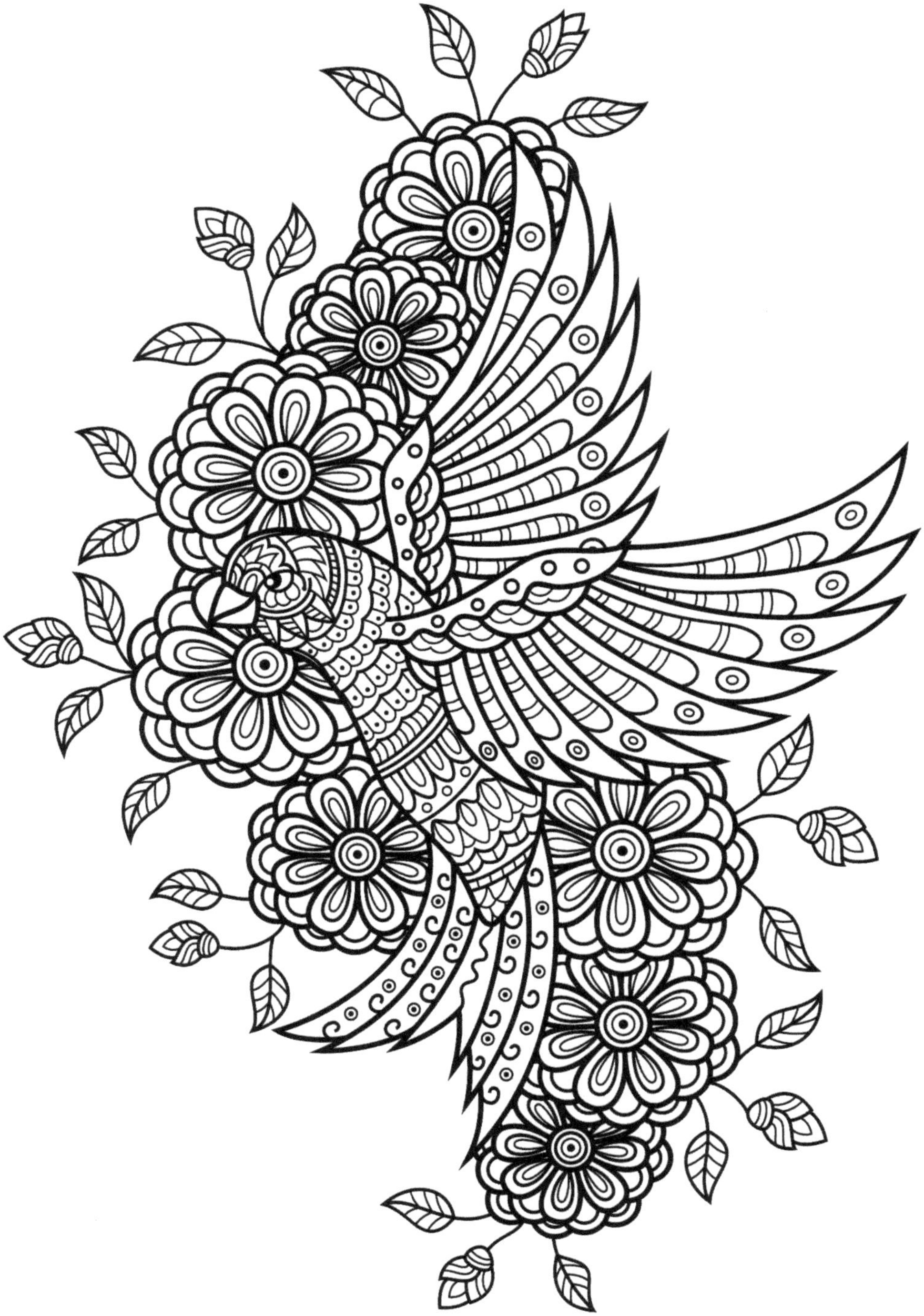

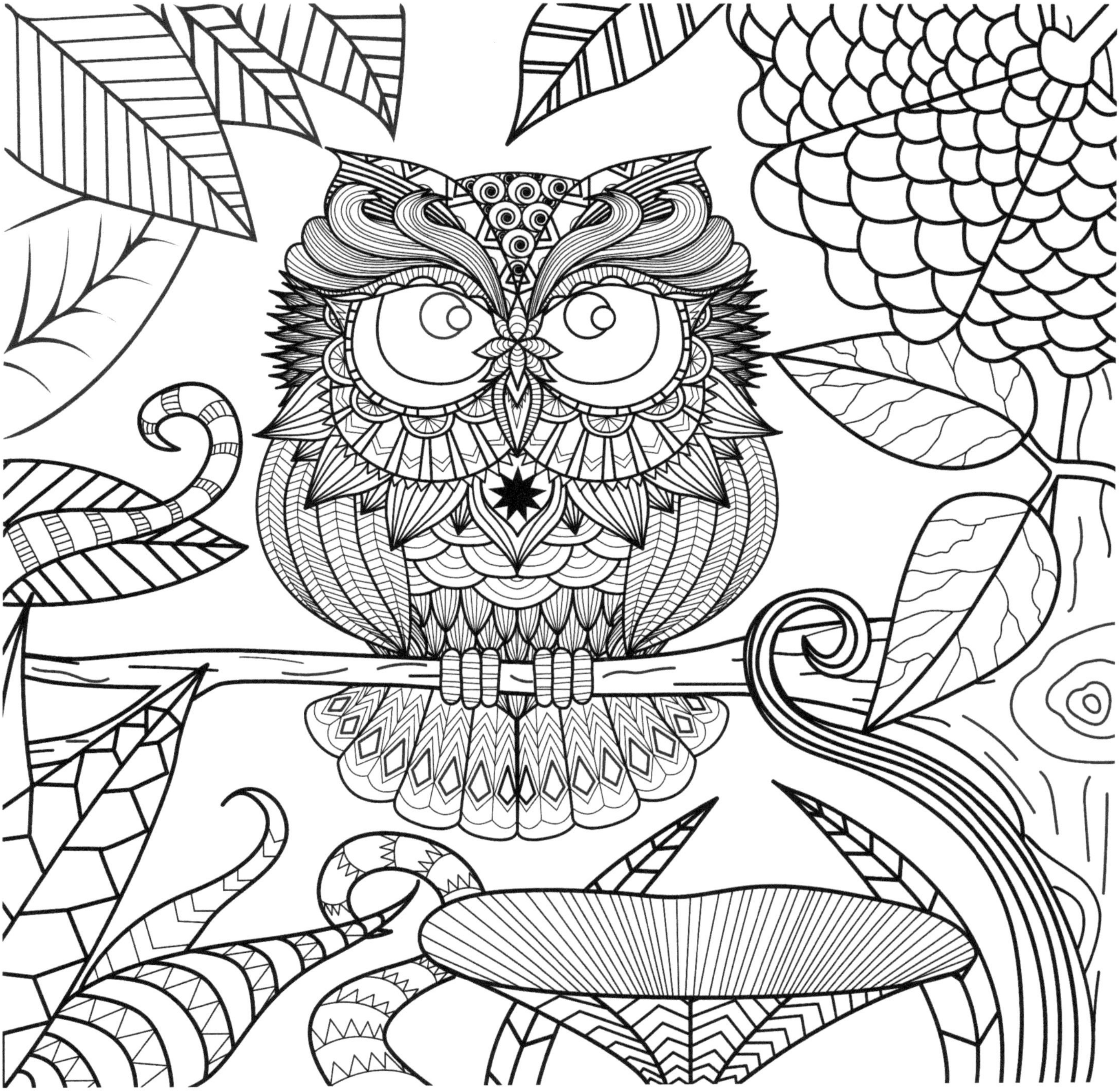

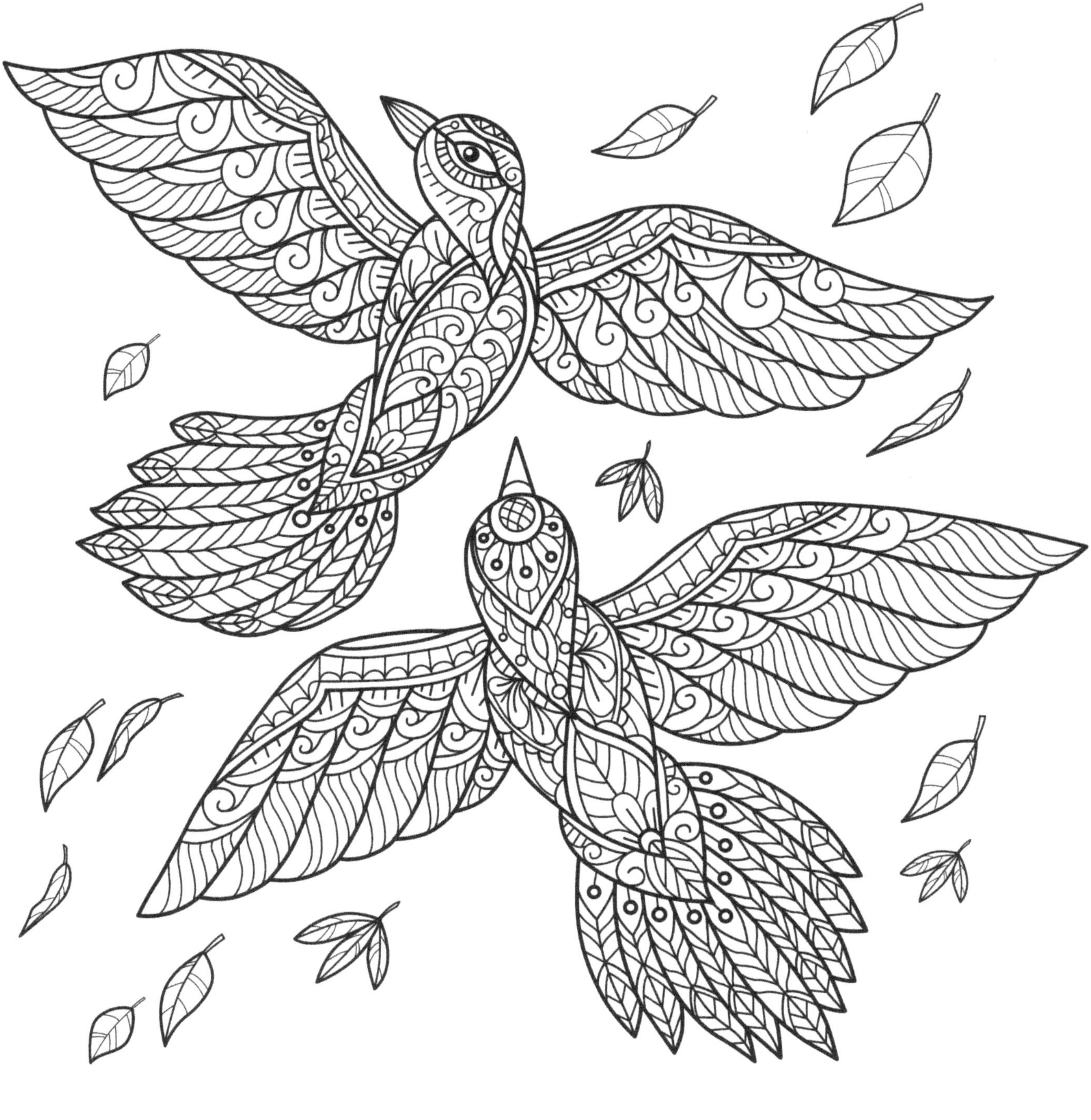

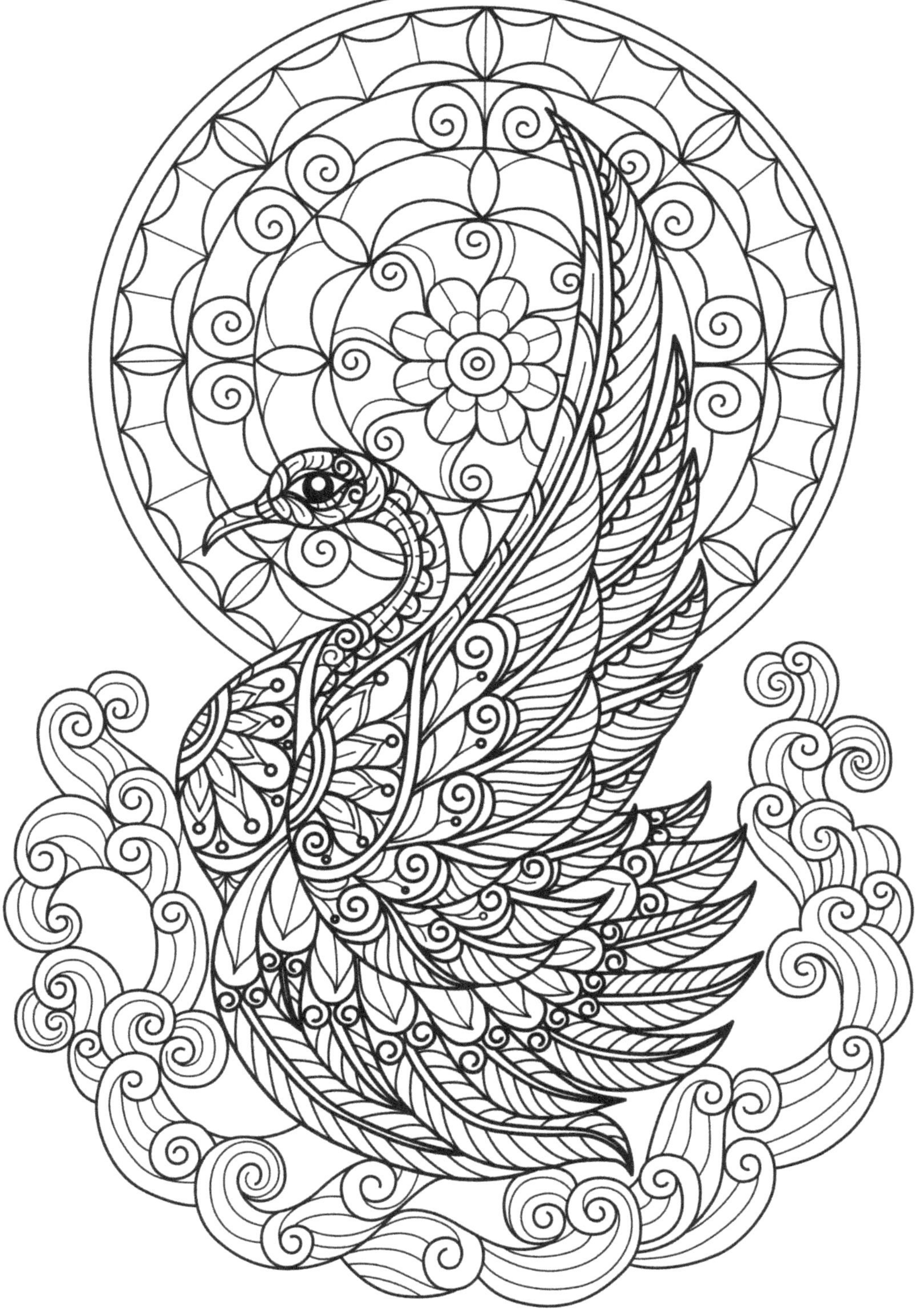

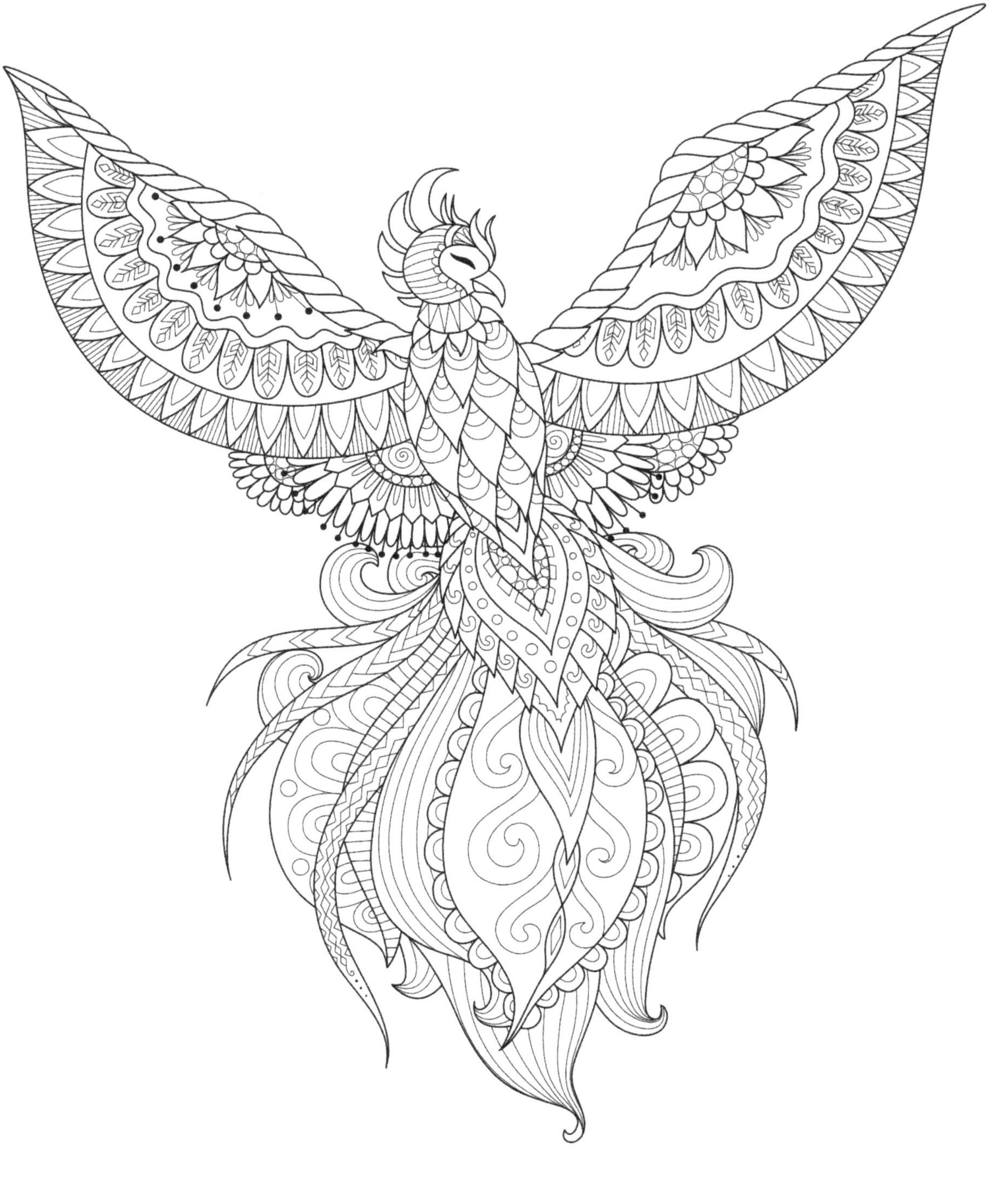

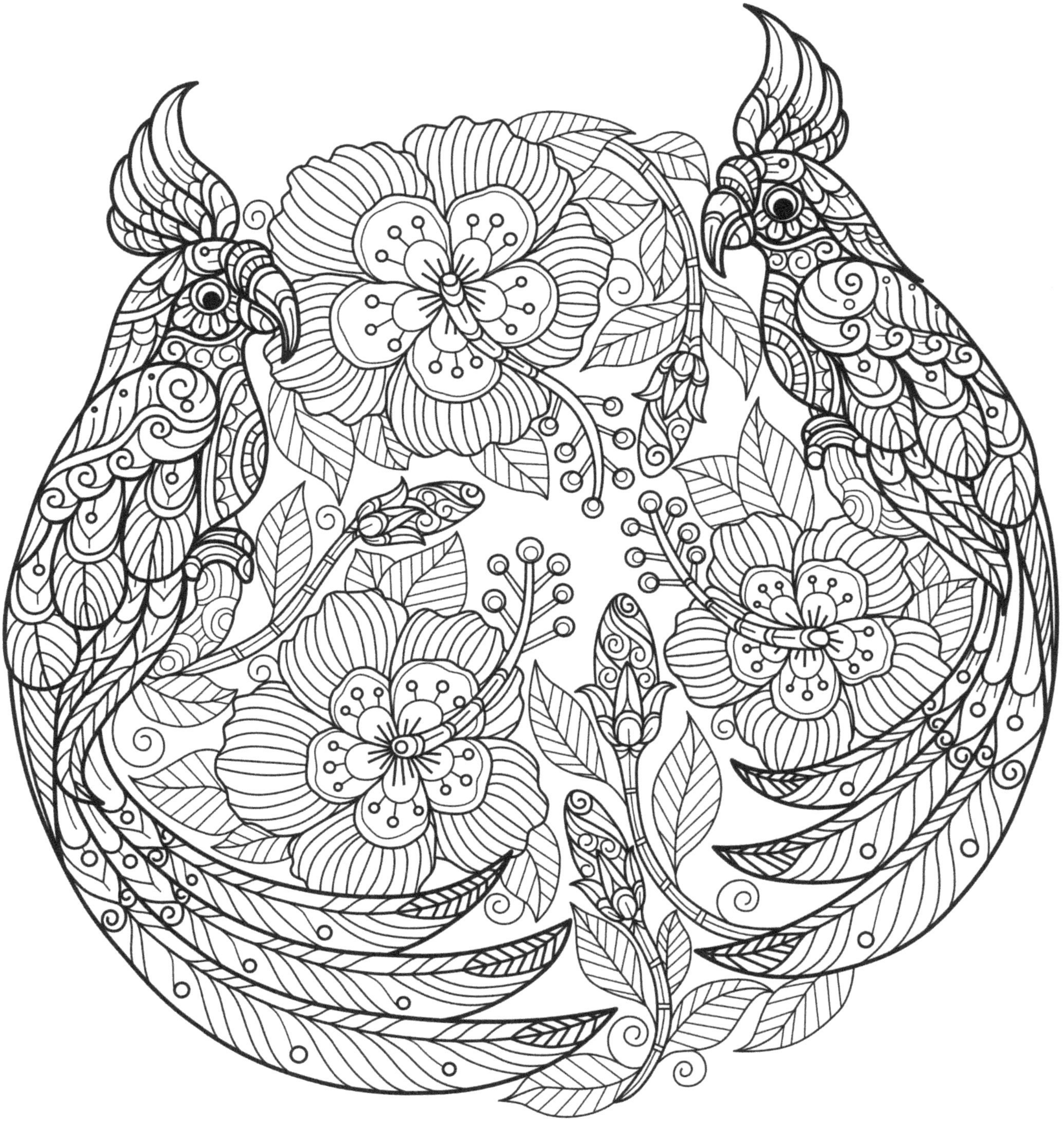

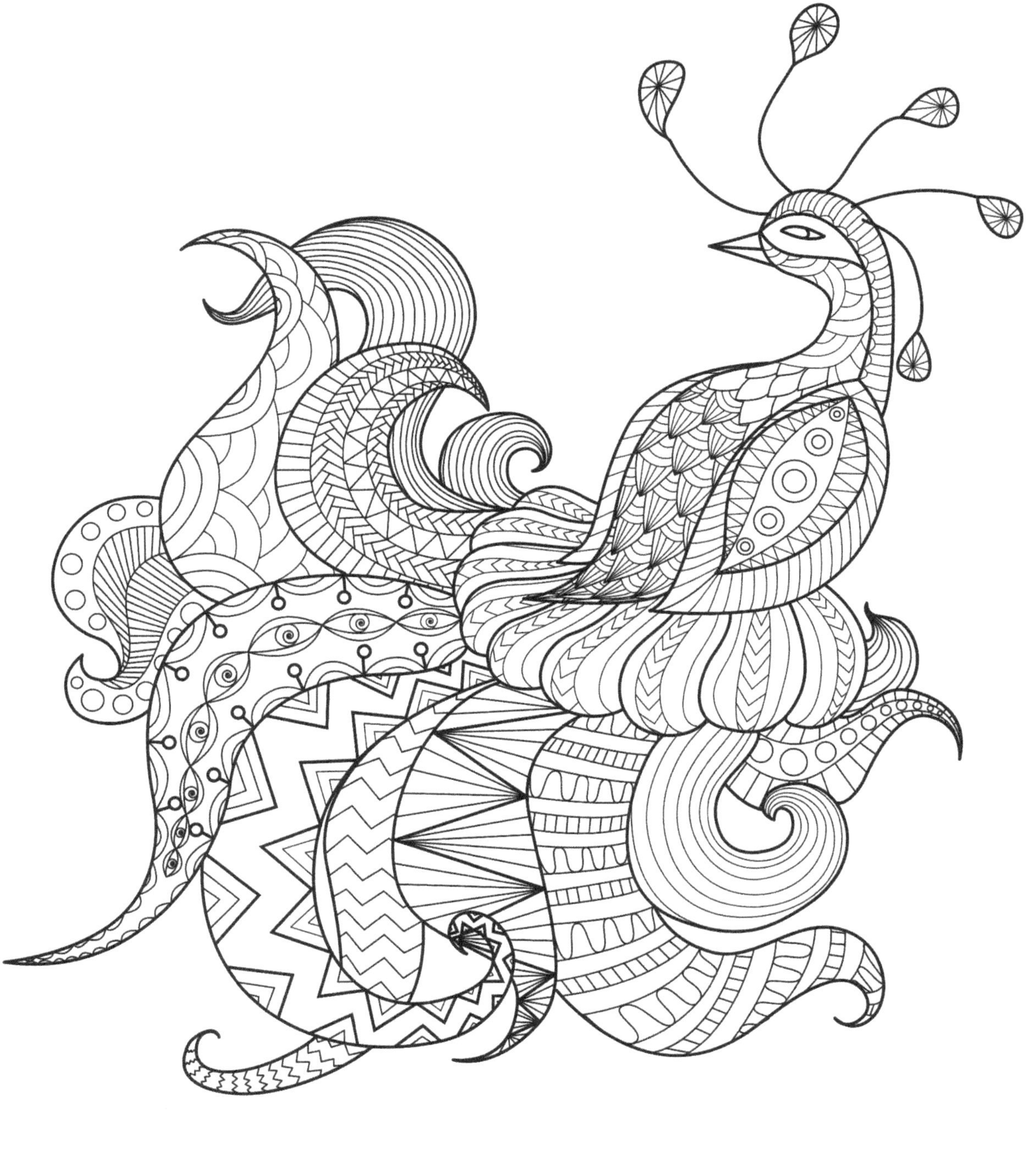

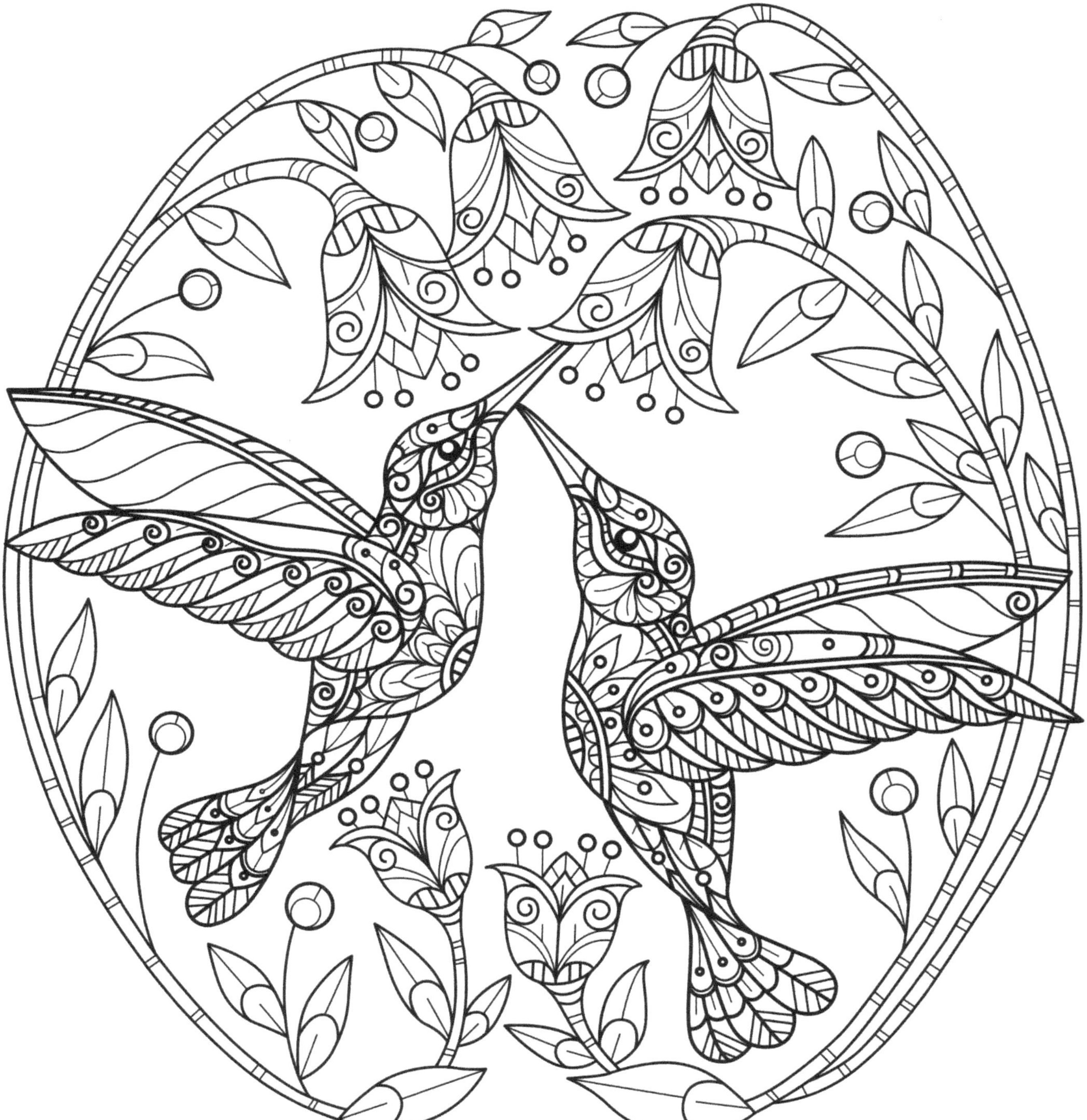

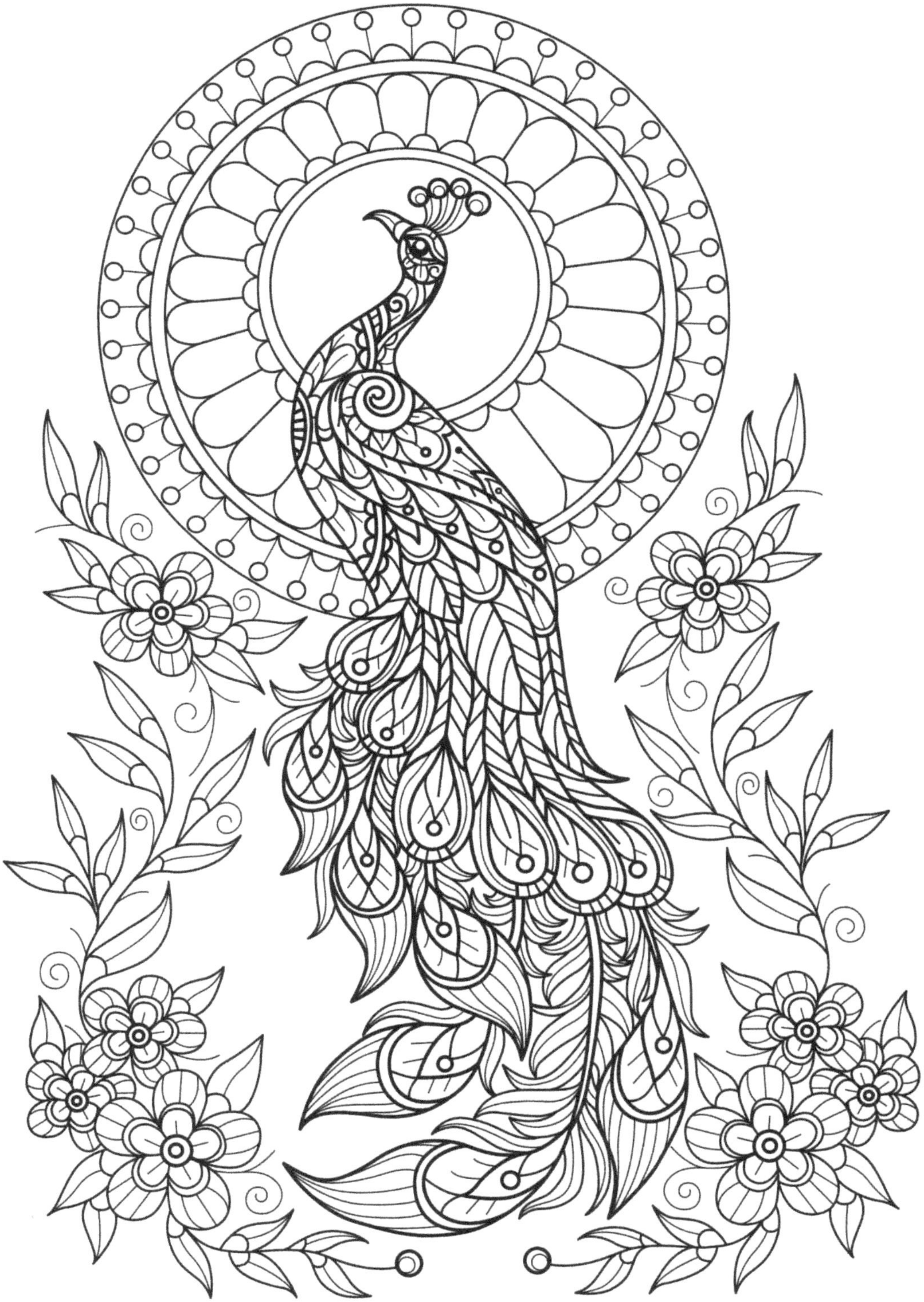

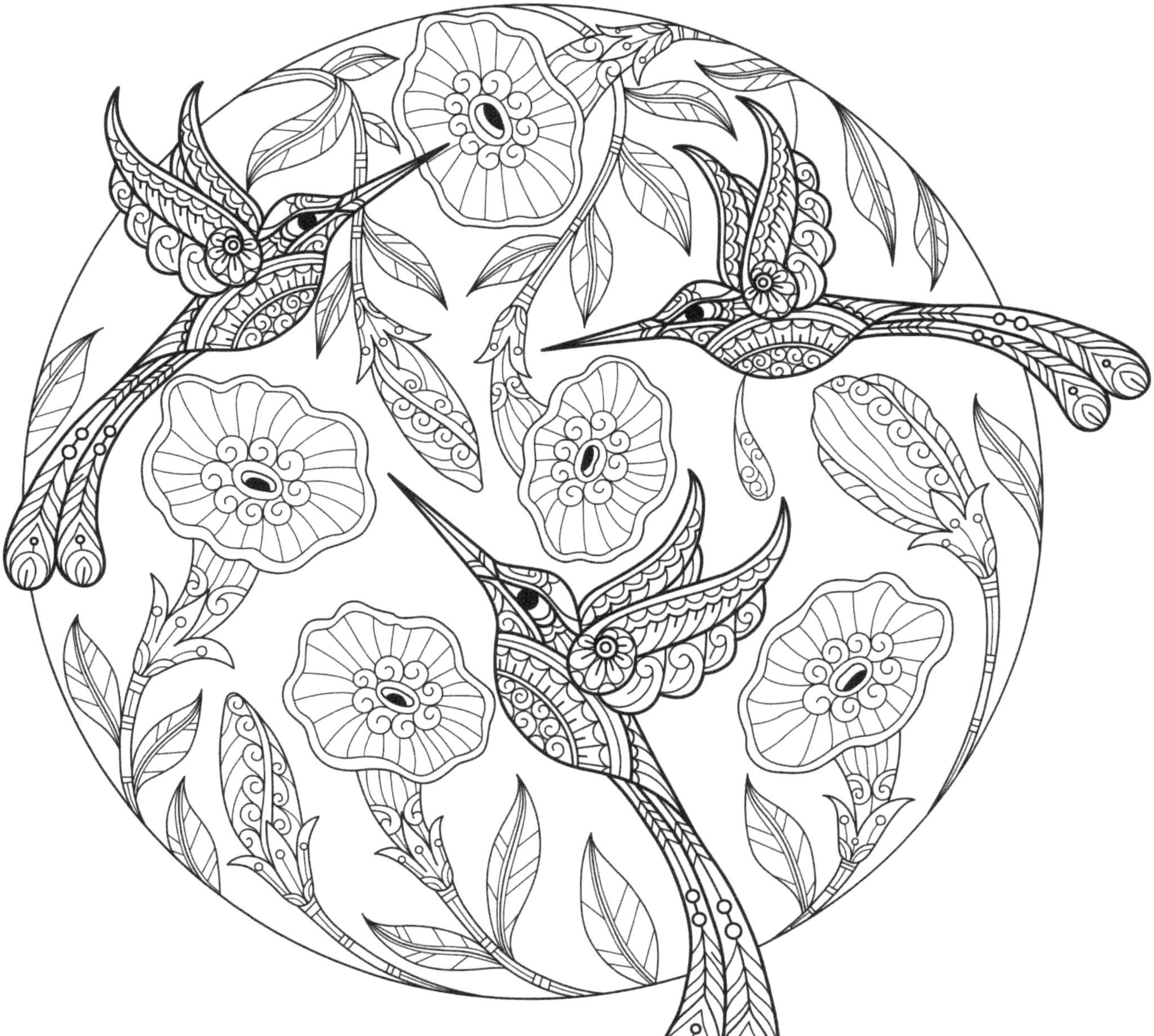

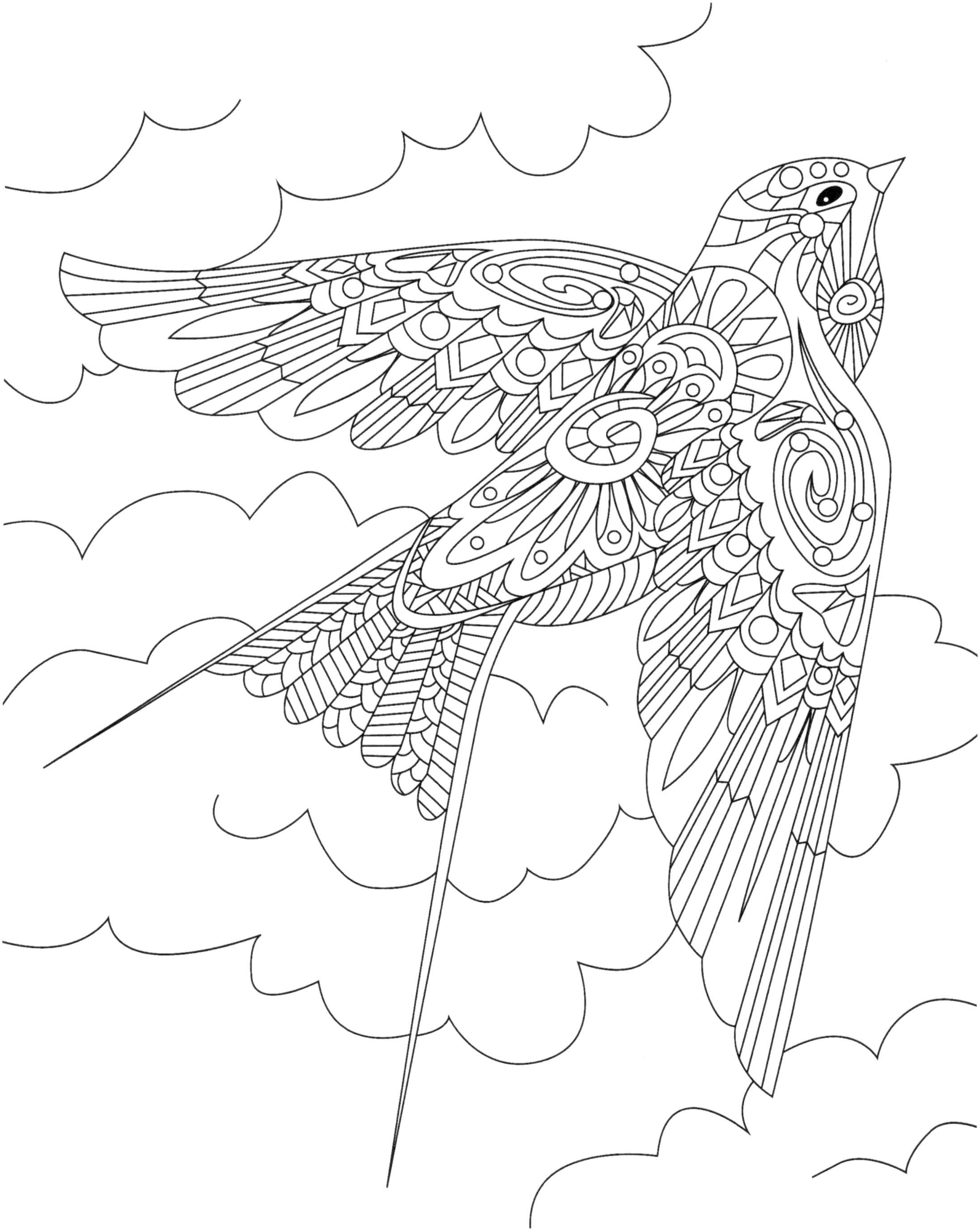

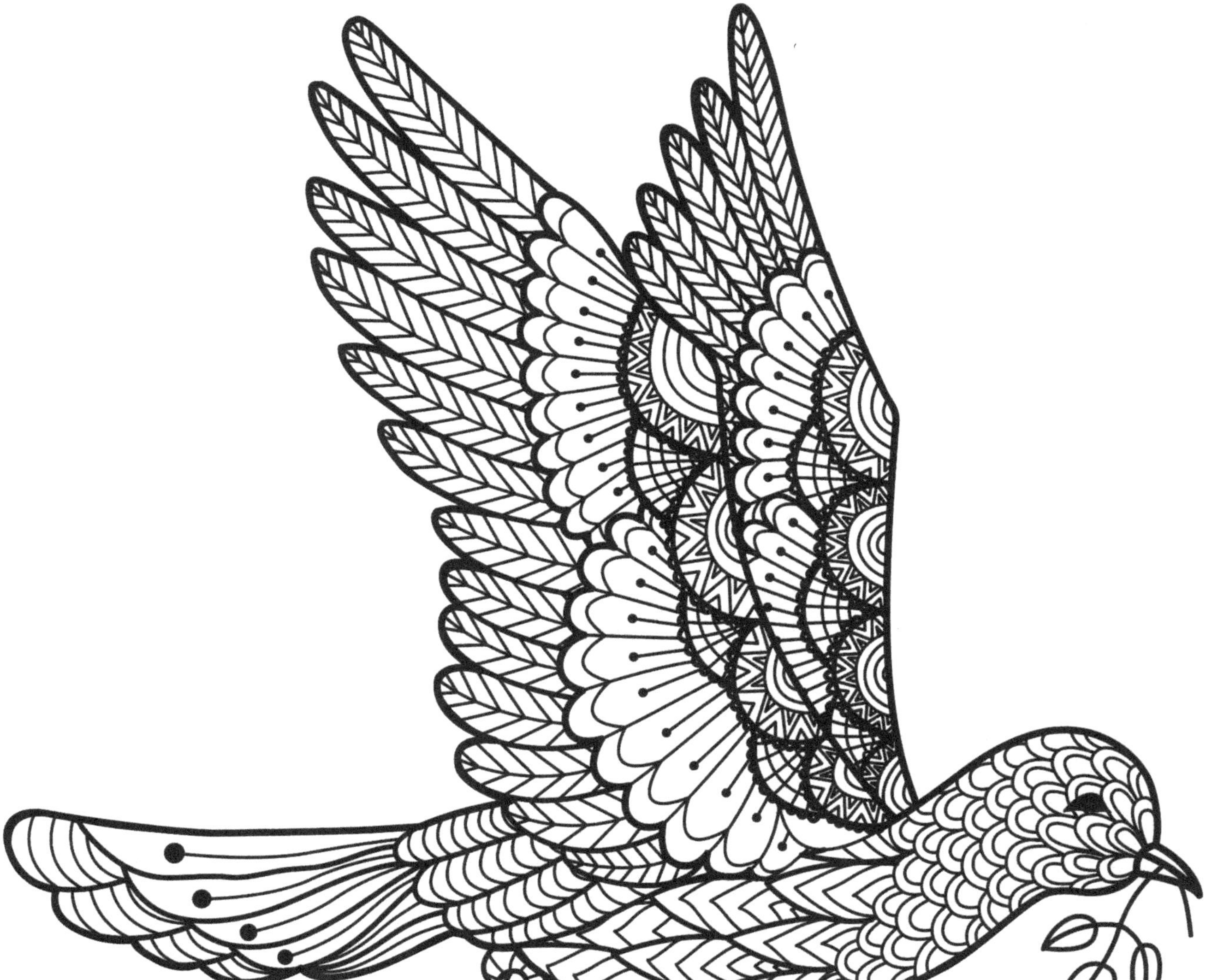

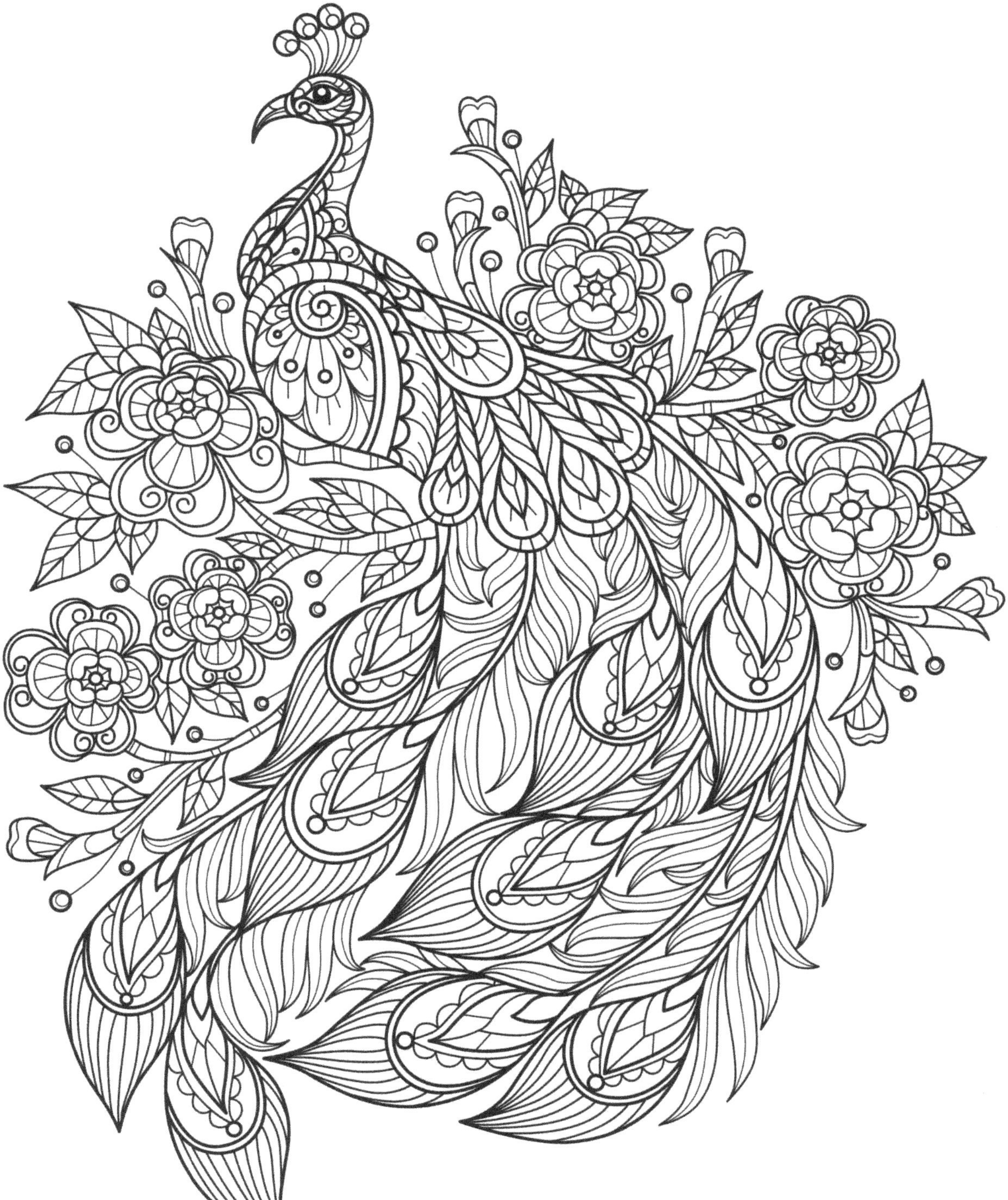

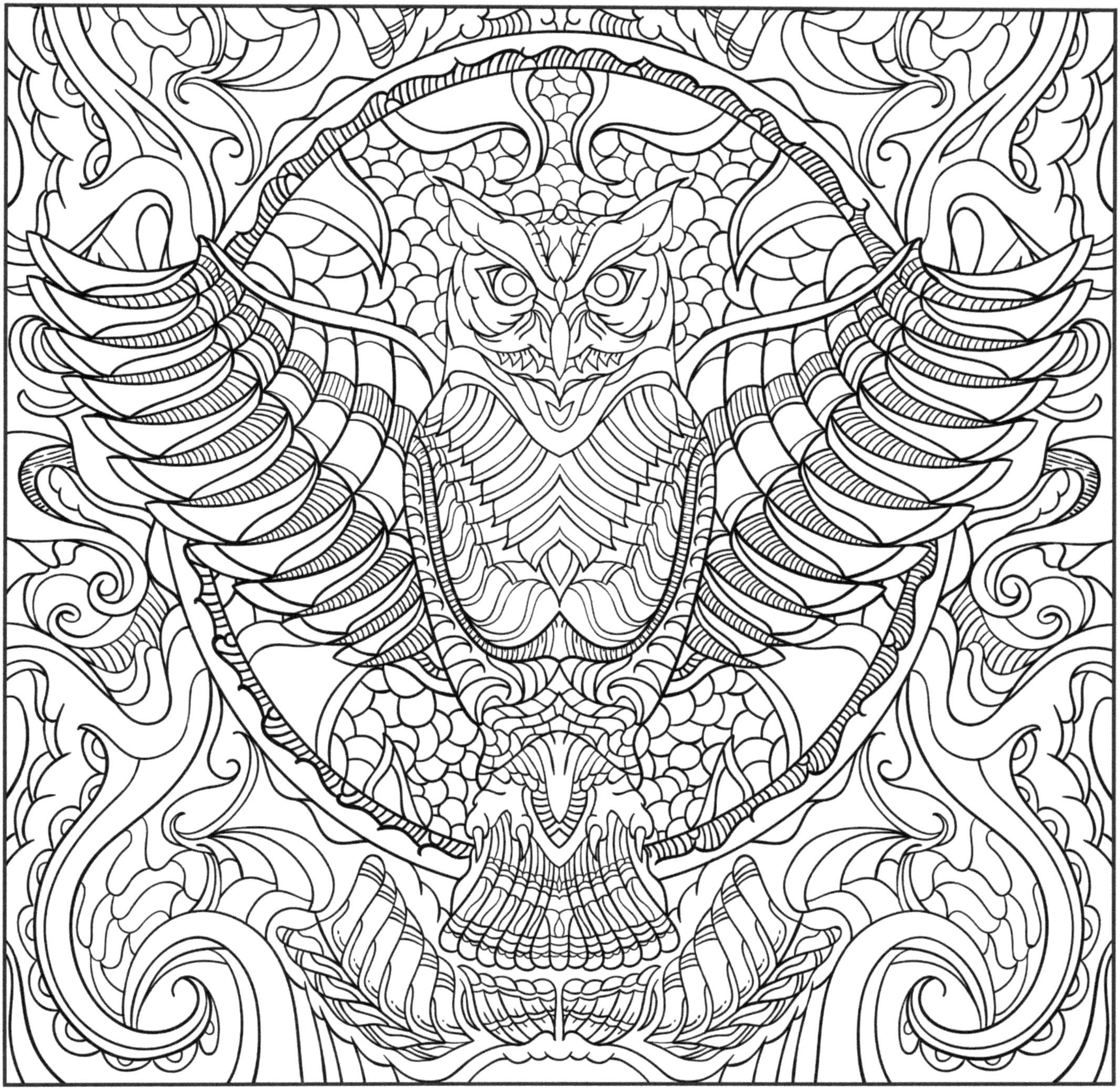

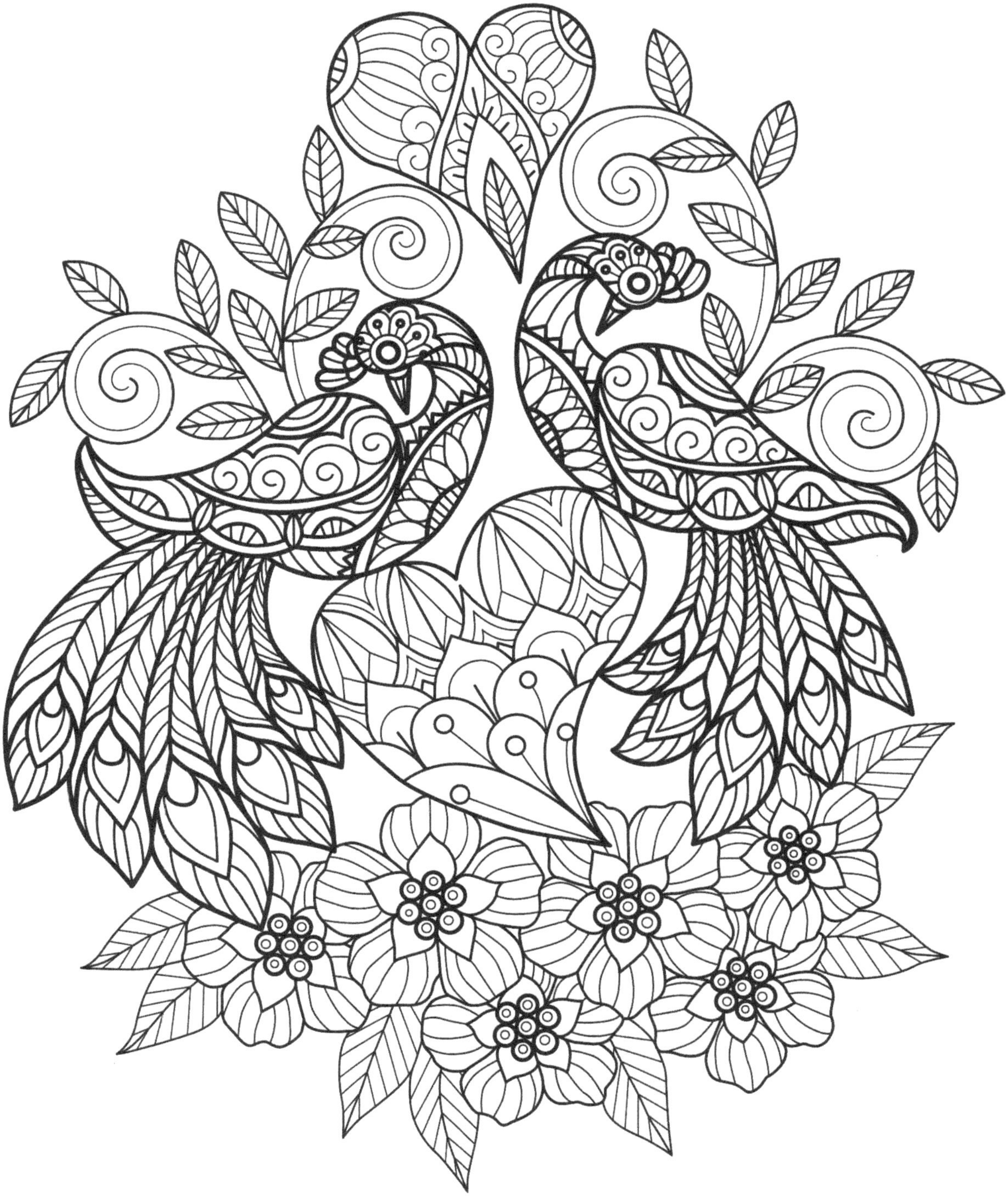

CPSIA information can be obtained
at www.ICGtesting.com
Printed in the USA
LVHW021527270723
753395LV00008B/175

9 798211 098930